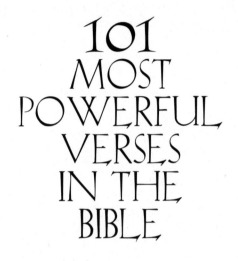

101 MOST POWERFUL VERSES IN THE BIBLE

101
MOST
POWERFUL
VERSES
IN THE
BIBLE

Steve and Lois Rabey

WARNER
Faith

A Division of AOL Time Warner Book Group

Unless otherwise noted, all Scripture quotations are from the HOLY BIBLE: NEW INTERNA-TIONAL VERSION®. Copyright © 1973, 1978, 1984 by International Bible Society. Used by permission of Zondervan Bible Publishers. All rights reserved.

Scripture quotations noted NLT are from the *Holy Bible,* New Living Translation, copyright © 1996. Used by permission of Tyndale House Publishers, Inc., Wheaton, Illinois 60189. All rights reserved.

Warner Books, Inc. 1271 Avenue of the Americas, New York, NY 10020.

Visit our website at www.twbookmark.com

⦿ **WARNER**𝓕𝒶𝒾𝓉𝓱   A Division of AOL Time Warner Book Group

Warner Faith is a trademark of Warner Books Inc.

Printed in the United States of America

First Warner Books Printing: February 2004

10   9   8   7   6   5   4   3   2   1

Library of Congress Cataloging-in-Publication Data

Rabey, Steve.
    101 most powerful verses in the Bible / Steve Rabey and Lois Rabey.
        p.cm.
    ISBN 0-446-53216-9
    1. Bible—Criticism, interpretation, etc. I. Title: One hundred and one most powerful verses in the Bible. II. Title: One hundred one most powerful verses in the Bible. III. Rabey, Lois Mowday. IV. Title.

BS538.R25 2004
220.6—dc22   2003057621

We dedicate this book to Justin, Alex, Lisa, Brady, Nathan, Cole, and Dylan.

We dedicate this book to Justin, Alex, Lisa, Brady, Nathan, Cole, and Dylan.

Acknowledgments

Writing this book has given us an opportunity to parcel out some of the Biblical knowledge we've accumulated over the years from books, sermons, and other sources. Thanking everyone who has helped us would be both impossible and impractical, but that doesn't mean we don't appreciate it.

Family members and friends have provided many of the stories found in the pages that follow, and we thank them for sharing their lives with us.

Thanks also to Greg Johnson at Alive Communications and our friends at Warner Faith: Rolf Zettersten, Leslie Peterson, and Steve Wilburn.

Contents

General Editors' Preface

There are thousands of verses in the Bible. How can we find the specific verses containing the eternal wisdom and divine guidance that will help each one of us grow deeper spiritually and live more faithfully? This book and others in The 101 Most Powerful series will help you find and unlock powerful passages of Scripture that inspire, comfort, and challenge.

The *101 Most Powerful Prayers in the Bible* helps us open our hearts to God by showing us how earlier saints and sinners prayed.

The *101 Most Powerful Promises in the Bible* brings together those passages that convey God's boundless and eternal love for his creation and his creatures.

The *101 Most Powerful Proverbs in the Bible* will enable us to apply God's timeless truths to many of the messy details of daily life.

And *101 Most Powerful Verses in the Bible* provides a treasury of divine insight gathered from nearly every book of the Old and New Testaments.

This and the other books in this series will never replace the Bible, but we do hope they will help you grasp its powerful and life-changing lessons and better utilize its wisdom in your life.

Talented writers made editing this series a breeze. And working on this volume has been more fun than writing a book should be (we know, having written thirty others).

After scanning our personal memory banks and flipping through the pages of some of our most heavily worn Bibles in search of those verses that have meant the most to us over the years, we tried to unlock their power and meaning for you as best we could. Though these verses were familiar to us, we found they still had much to teach us. We hope you feel the same way as you read the pages that follow.

Steve and Lois Rabey

Introduction:
You Can Experience God's Power

Ocean waves batter the shore. In the heavens, lightning explodes and thunder roars. And deep in the forest, the roots of an ancient tree cut through solid rock, slowly turning it into dust.

Every day all around our globe, events like these demonstrate the power of God through nature. We can also witness God's eternal and infinite power in more gentle acts of creation and change. A beautiful flower pushes its way up through a late spring snow. A tiny bird diligently pecks his way out of his own hard shell. A newborn baby cries as those who encircle her look on in grateful wonder.

There is yet another place where we can see God's power in all its glory: in the Bible, which is the revealed Word of God. Here's how the apostle Paul put it: "For the message of the cross is foolishness to those who are perishing, but to us who are being saved it is the power of God" (1 Cor. 1:18).

All of us can experience more of God's power if we study and meditate on the Bible. Just as a hydroelectric dam converts water pressure into electricity, God's Word transforms our lives into conduits for his power.

Over the centuries, people have devised a dizzying variety of techniques for trying to understand God and discover his power. One of the oldest approaches is to consult the stars—a method many still use today. Throughout the ages, people have also conferred with gods and oracles, cut up the intestines of animals, flipped coins, or offered human sacrifices in an effort to receive supernatural inspiration.

Christianity has a much more direct approach. From its ancient origins in the Jewish faith, Christianity has taught two important truths: God exists, and he communicates his will to his children. Instead of waiting for us to find him, God has taken the initiative and reached out to us.

In the Hebrew Bible or Old Testament, he spoke through patriarchs, prophets, and poets. In the New Testament, he spoke more clearly than ever before through his only Son, Jesus Christ, and through some of Jesus' closest disciples.

Whether you call it divine revelation, Holy Scripture, God's Word, or simply the Bible, the message is the same: God cares about us so much that he has given us a book that tells us what he is like and how we can have a loving relationship with him.

During the first twenty centuries of Christian history, people have turned to the Bible for wisdom so they can make sound decisions and live godly lives. They have scanned its pages for encouragement so they can endure life's hard times. And they have trusted its teachings as a source of solid spiritual truth in a world of competing creeds and doctrines.

Still, the Bible isn't always easy to navigate or understand. Covering thousands of years, taking up hundreds of pages, and subdivided into sixty-six books, almost twelve hundred chapters, and more than thirty thousand verses, the Bible can seem big, intimidating, and confusing.

For some of us, reading the Bible is like trying to make sense out of the user's manual that comes with a new DVD player. After slogging through a few pages of technical mumbo jumbo, we find our eyes glazing over, our brains shutting down, and our hands beginning to twitch.

Some people may be tempted to throw manuals like this across the room in anger and disgust. Those blessed with abundant physical strength may want to tear them to shreds. But most of us simply put hard-to-decipher books on a shelf where they sit unread and quietly gather dust.

If that's what you're doing with your Bible, you're missing out on the world's most treasured source of insight, inspiration, and power.

In the pages that follow, we have done some of the research and legwork for you, highlighting 101 key verses that communicate God's will in clear and compelling ways. Here we cut through some of the questions people often ask when they read the Bible.

We certainly are not offering up our own book as a replacement for God's Word. Rather, we hope that as you read about the *101 Most Powerful Verses* you will be even more hungry to dive into the remaining riches of God's Word and discover for yourself what they have to offer.

This is a collaborative work, with each of us writing about half of the 101 readings. Many of the readings use first-person pronouns. That's because we thought it would be more effective to use the singular "I" instead of the plural "we" when providing personal anecdotes. In some cases it will be clear who is speaking, but in most of the others it won't make that much difference whether it's Steve or Lois.

Each reading closes with a brief prayer that we've designed to help guide you into God's loving presence. Our prayer is that as you study the readings in this book, you will grow in your knowledge of God's Word and begin experiencing more of what Paul called the "power of [Christ's] resurrection" (Phil. 3:10).

101
MOST
POWERFUL
VERSES
IN THE
BIBLE

1

A Light in the Dark

*Your word is a lamp to my feet
and a light for my path.*

Psalm 119:105

For little children, darkness can bring about feelings of anxiety and fear. Darkness can harm adults, too, making us lose our way and exposing us to danger.

I know hikers who have been forced to sleep out in the wilds of the Rocky Mountains after the sun quickly set and darkness engulfed any signs of a trail. Those hardy souls who are adventurous enough to brave Alaska's frigid winters encounter more than their share of darkness. The sun doesn't shine for days at a time, leaving hikers unusually vulnerable and bringing disorder to those huddled safely inside who are desperately trying to figure out if it is morning or evening.

Closer to home, even a brief power outage can turn a familiar room into a potential disaster area full of obstacles that seem to lurch out at your shins or your head. And who among us hasn't experienced the momentary frights that can occur when we are awoken by an unusual noise in the hallway during a pitch-black night?

A missionary I know once told me about a South American tribe whose members traveled only at night. In order to keep from losing their way or falling off of one of their region's many cliffs, the men and women of this tribe lit tiny candles that they carried on strings. The candles provided enough illumination for only the next step or two, but that was enough.

Our lives often seem like pilgrimages on rough trails winding through dark and dangerous lands. But God's Word is like a candle that clarifies our path and shows us the way to go.

There are many books in the world, but only one stands supreme. The Bible is God's matchless revelation to us. Since the invention of the printing press more than five centuries ago, the Bible has been the world's best-selling book.

For millennia people copied its contents onto papyrus, parchment, and paper so they could share its wise words with others. Scholars and missionaries have translated its message into hundreds of languages. Brave souls have risked their lives to spread its message or even gone to their deaths rather than deny its teachings.

Why have so many people made such a fuss about this one book for such a long, long time? As the verse from Psalm 119 suggests, the Bible is a source of certain light in an often dark and confusing world.

Psalm 119, which is the longest single chapter in the entire Bible, gives plenty of other reasons people throughout the ages have turned to this unique book. Titled "In praise of God's Word," the psalm lists benefits that come from studying and applying the Bible: it helps us walk in accordance with God's law; it encourages us to remain steadfast and pure; it teaches us to distinguish truth from falsehood and right from wrong; and it strengthens weary souls, bringing hope, comfort, and courage.

George Fox was an English preacher during the seventeenth cen-

tury and the founder of the Society of Friends, or Quakers. In one of his many sermons, he told his listeners about the light of God's love: "I saw also that there was an ocean of darkness and death, but an infinite ocean of light and love which flowed over the ocean of darkness."

God has given us the Bible, and with its illumination, we can confound the darkness of our world.

————

God, thank you for sharing your Word with us. May its words find a home in my heart and light my way.

2

The Creator of All That Is

In the beginning God created the heavens and the earth.

Genesis 1:1

THESE familiar opening words of the Bible proclaim the most amazing of God's many powers. He is the Creator of all that exists. And he created it out of nothing.

I find that truth difficult to comprehend. My own life is full of incomplete tasks that are evidence of my inability to understand simple instructions, much less comprehend the magnificence of a God who made everything without instructions, raw materials, or others to help him.

As a young wife and mother I decided to learn to sew. My mother had been a wonderful seamstress, but I had been interested in more active endeavors and was seldom inside watching her craft the dresses and suits I loved wearing. Her creations were touched with imaginative details and made from the most stylish linens and silks of the day.

When I walked into the fabric store I was hopeful that attempting much more simple styles would promise success, even to a novice like me.

The saleslady was helpful and assured me that with easy patterns I would be able to make darling dresses for my two little girls. An hour later I left the store with all the supplies I needed and headed home to dust off the sewing machine that I had inherited from my mother.

It didn't take long for frustration to set in. Confusing instructions filled the flimsy pattern paper: "Cut on the bias," "Gather the sleeve," "Match the notches on facings." I did complete those early projects but the results were less than stellar.

Fortunately, there are other complex tasks I can comprehend and perform. And millions of people in our world have achieved greatness in their abilities to accomplish innumerable feats. Man-made inventions and human discoveries reveal the wonders of the mind and spill into our lives at a pace that's dizzying.

Even so, none of them even begin to compare with what God has done, and we all can see our own limitations when measured against his handiwork. We stand in awe of the complexity of the world in which we live and believe the truth of Genesis 1:1.

But not everyone believes as we believe. Numerous explanations appear in textbooks and claim superiority over the assertion that a power we know as God called life into being. Finite and rational minds grapple with the complexities of the world around them and seek ways to explain definitively how our world began.

But we who believe him and the biblical account of creation marvel at the power and majesty of our Creator. Our acceptance doesn't diminish the wonder of God's work but leaves room for the mystery of it.

———

Father, we worship you with amazement as we bask in the beauty of your creation. Thank you for all you have made.

3

Be Ready

Therefore keep watch, because you do not know the day or the hour.

Matthew 25:13

CHRISTIANS have argued for centuries about when and how Christ is going to return to the earth and usher in the end of time—a scenario a number of books in the Bible have predicted.

"This generation is going to see the climax of history as predicted by the prophets," said a man named Hal Lindsey, the most famous end-times author of the twentieth century. Lindsey's 1970 book, *The Late Great Planet Earth*, has sold 30 million copies and helped put the fear of God into many readers who wondered if they were ready for Christ's return.

Over the years, end-times authors have developed an amazing number of schemes for trying to figure out what complex passages in the Old Testament Book of Daniel and the New Testament Book of Revelation mean.

For Lindsey, the Armageddon clock began ticking in 1948 with the creation of the state of Israel. He originally predicted that the second coming of Christ would occur no later than 1988.

Lindsey wasn't the first person to pick a specific date for the Second Coming. Over the years, detailed predictions have come from the Shakers, Alexander Campbell and the Disciples of Christ, William Miller and the Seventh-day Adventists, Calvary Chapel founder Chuck Smith, television evangelist Jack Van Impe, and author Edgar C. Whisenant, who wrote a book entitled *88 Reasons the Rapture Will Be in 88*. And many Christians thought the Y2K computer glitch would usher in the end of the world. *USA Today* reported that "as many as 100" end-times books and novels would be published in the year leading up to January 1, 2000.

Somehow we're still here, and all the end-times authors are busily revising their dates. But if anything, interest in the end times has only grown. The bestselling Left Behind novels by Tim LaHaye and Jerry Jenkins have done more than their share to inspire a whole new wave of apocalyptic speculation. The novels show the chaos and confusion that could result after Christians have been "raptured" (or taken from the earth) and sinners try to survive in a world now dominated by the Antichrist. (Some Christian thinkers have criticized the books' interpretation of theology, but that hasn't slowed their massive popularity. According to Tyndale House, which publishes the series, the Left Behind novels and related books have sold some 50 million copies.)

But many of the well-meaning Christians who have focused so much time and attention on the Second Coming seem to have missed one important point. Christ himself told us that we should concentrate not on the day and the hour of his return but on the state of our souls.

Keeping watch means living our lives in such a way that if Christ returned today, he would find us pleasing in his sight. If I knew I would face Jesus before the sun went down, I think I might start by confessing my sins to God, my family, my co-workers, and my next door neighbors, seeking their forgiveness for past wrongs. I would make some phone calls to loved ones to express my concern for them and share the message of Christ's love. If time allowed, I might even examine my checkbook to make sure I have fulfilled financial commitments made earlier to churches and charities.

It means doing everything we can with the time, energy, and resources we have to extend the kingdom of God—both through sharing the gospel of Christ with others and working to see our culture embrace godly values of justice and righteousness.

And it means being faithful to Christ on a moment-by-moment basis, regardless of whether Christ comes back the next minute or long after we have died.

———

Father, help me avoid end-times paranoia and instead develop full-time preparedness for your return.

4

The Greatest Commandment

Hear O Israel: The LORD our God, the LORD is one. Love the LORD your God with all your heart and with all your soul and with all your strength.

Deuteronomy 6:4–5

JESUS doesn't call people to a social or political movement, or even to a life of religion or ethical living. More than anything, he calls us to love God—a call that the laws of Moses first stated.

Repeatedly throughout his earthly ministry, Jesus called this the greatest commandment. "God is love," affirmed John the Apostle. "Whoever lives in love lives in God, and God in him" (1 John 4:16).

Centuries later, Protestant theologians restated this simple call to love God. "What is the chief end of man?" asked the 1646 Westminster Confession of Faith. "Man's chief end is to glorify God, and to enjoy Him for ever."

Throughout Christian history, many disciples of Jesus have described the immense love of God. Perhaps none did so as eloquently as Saint Bernard of Clairvaux (1090–1153), a Cistercian monk who was both an intellectual and a mystic, and whose French monastery had a worldwide influence. Bernard's most famous work is *On Loving God*, which contains the following words of wisdom:

> You want me to tell you why God is to be loved and how much. I answer, the reason for loving God is God Himself; and the measure of love due to Him is immeasurable love. Is this plain?
>
> We are to love God for Himself, because of a twofold reason; nothing is more reasonable, nothing more profitable. When one asks, Why should I love God? he may mean, What is lovely in God? or What shall I gain by loving God? In either case, the same sufficient cause of love exists, namely, God Himself.

Bernard argued that God is entitled to our wholehearted affection:

> For although God would be loved without respect of reward, yet He wills not to leave love unrewarded. True charity cannot be left destitute, even though she is unselfish and seeketh not her own (1 Corinthians 13:5).
>
> Love is an affection of the soul, not a contract: it cannot rise from a mere agreement, nor is it so to be gained. It is spontaneous in its origin and impulse; and true love is its own satisfaction. It has its reward; but that reward is the object beloved. For whatever you seem to love, if it is on account of something else, what you do really love is that something else, not the apparent object of desire.[1]

God could have created robots that would "love" him on command, but he didn't. He gave us hearts and free will to do with as we please. Still, as Bernard told us so eloquently, love is our only appropriate response to God.

———

I love you, Father. Help my love for you to grow.

5

We Are on Dry Ground

And the Israelites went through the sea on dry ground, with a wall of
water on their right and on their left.

Exodus 14:22

PERHAPS many young moviegoers today have missed Cecil B. De-
Mille's 1956 cinematic depiction of the parting of the Red Sea as
the Israelites fled from Pharaoh's army. Were they to see *The Ten
Commandments* in one of its numerous television reruns, they might
wonder how this movie received an Academy Award for Best Special
Effects.

Charlton Heston as an aging Moses holds an outstretched arm
over the parting water as the sea rolls up into two huge waves on
either side of the Israelites. While the superimposed images of the
tumultuous waters don't generate the *Wow!* response viewers experience in so many movies today, they do convey that a miracle was
taking place.

I saw *The Ten Commandments* several times, and I always marveled at
the parting waters and never once took notice of the dry ground Exodus 14:22 mentions. Why does the Bible even give us this information?

I think we, like the Israelites, often forget that God has placed us on a firm foundation.

The Israelites were God's chosen people. He was in the course of taking them out of Egypt and into the promised land, but they started complaining as soon as they saw Pharaoh's army pursuing them. In their fear, their faith faltered. They grumbled to Moses, saying they would rather have died in Egypt than out in the desert (Exod. 14:11). How soon they seemed to forget the terrible slavery they had suffered under the hand of Pharaoh.

Despite their grumbling, God took the Israelites safely to the other side of the Red Sea and destroyed Pharaoh's army by causing the waves to collapse on them. The Israelites had traveled on dry ground.

Imagine thousands of people, animals, carts, and wagons struggling through the muck had God not supernaturally dried up the seabed. Their progress would have been slow and perhaps altogether impossible.

I think the reminder for us in this verse is that God's power holds us firmly on the dry ground of his love, no matter what is happening in our lives. We may feel threatened by the waves of life. We may not feel as if we are secure, but we are. Our spiritual feet may feel mired in the slush of uncomfortable circumstances, but God's presence in our lives keeps us going.

Just as the Israelites were God's people, we who believe in his Son are his people. Sometimes his power is evident in our lives in spectacular ways as the parting of the Red Sea was in Exodus. At other times, we experience God's power in almost unnoticeable ways, such as the ground being dry when the Israelites crossed it.

God's most dramatic rescue in my own life unfolded in the years immediately following my first husband's death. I was thirty-four years old with two daughters, age seven and ten. My husband and I went to high school together, and I couldn't remember what it felt like to live without him. Many of my friends remarked that they fully expected to see me carried into my home on a stretcher when returning from the scene of the hot-air balloon accident that claimed his life.

Instead, the evidence of God's grace and provision was amazing. I experienced a confidence that God would "part the waters" for us and was able to focus on our future in ways that can only be explained as miraculous. I went from being a homemaker who relied heavily on my husband to being the sole adult in our household. Like Moses, I stepped into the water and God dried up the muddy ground.

Whether we notice it or not, the power is there. Whether we feel it or not, we are on dry ground.

———

Father, thank you that we rest on the firm foundation of relationship with Jesus Christ.

6

God's Purifying Stream

If we confess our sins, he is faithful and just and will forgive us our sins and purify us from all unrighteousness.

1 John 1:9

SHAME on you!"

These three simple words still ring in my ears decades after they were shouted my way.

I don't remember the innocent adolescent behavior that led to my being scolded. But I know I'll never forget how I felt when one of the more rigorous older members of my church pointed her gloved finger at me and humiliated me in front of what seemed like the entire congregation.

These words of harsh judgment inflicted painful wounds. Worse yet, my pain caused me to make the following fateful pledge: *I will never again tell anyone about any of my faults or failures!*

From that point on, I began being less honest when I hurt someone, broke something, or fell short of a goal. I kept everything to myself and put all my energy into covering up.

Unfortunately, covering up my problems only added to my feelings of failure, inadequacy, and guilt.

It came as a great relief to read, "If we confess our sins, he is faithful and just and will forgive us our sins and purify us from all unrighteousness."

At first glance, the whole process seems simple: we confess; God forgives; and everyone lives happily ever after.

But real life isn't so clear-cut. Why does the promised freedom of forgiveness often seem elusive? Why does guilt continue to haunt and taunt us? Why do we confess the same sins again and again only to remain entrapped by them?

Perhaps we have misunderstood what John meant about confession. Real confession is more than a hurried recitation of our flaws and failures. It is work. It hurts. It demands self-examination. It transforms a trite utterance into a sorrowful awareness of the many ways our sinful behavior grieves the Holy Spirit.

Growing up, I felt closer to my mother than my father. Mom was firm and she taught me that my actions had consequences, but she always balanced punishment with love for me as a person.

Dad was a different story. Any wrongdoing on my part seemed to ignite his already short fuse, leading to a barrage of anger and unkind words that caused me to shrink in shame and fear.

God isn't like my father. When I expose my sins to God, my confession opens up the door to his forgiveness and cleansing. Instead of hiding my woundedness, I offer it up to him who brings the healing balm of forgiveness and purification. It is this forgiving power that can change us from within.

———

Father, thank you for the grace and forgiveness that motivate me to share my sins and failures with you instead of hiding them deep in my soul.

7

Opening the Book of Nature

For since the creation of the world God's invisible qualities—his eternal power and divine nature—have been clearly seen, being understood from what has been made, so that men are without excuse.

Romans 1:20

I N the last few decades of the twentieth century, people around the globe began to realize that humanity was hurting the earth. Some of these people joined the environmental movement, which sought to slow the pollution of the world's air and water.

But respect for the earth is an ancient concept that dates back to the dawn of human history. That's because Christians and Jews believe that a loving Creator God formed the cosmos. And as Paul indicated in the Romans passage, we can see characteristics of the Creator in all that he made.

No one saw this connection between Creator and creation more than a humble thirteenth-century saint named Francis of Assisi. Francis saw God's fingerprints all over the world, and he believed that even the animals were designed to praise the Creator in their own powerful way: "Every creature in heaven and on earth and in the depths of the sea should give God praise and glory and honor and blessing." The Italian holy man was named the patron saint of the environmental movement.

One day, Francis and some of his brothers were out walking when they came across a large tree full of doves, crows, and other birds. As one of his biographers reported, "Francis left his companions in the road and ran eagerly to the birds" and "humbly begged them to listen to the word of God."

The biographer even recorded a portion of Francis's brief sermon to his winged friends: "My brothers, birds, you should praise your Creator very much and always love him; he gave you feathers to clothe you, wings so that you can fly, and whatever else was necessary for you."[1]

Today, the image of Francis caring for birds appears in paintings, sculptures, and thousands of backyard bird feeders. And every fall, on the Sunday closest to Francis's October 4 feast day, churches around the world host a "blessing of the animals" ceremony. These churches turn into temporary zoos as members bring their birds, dogs, cats, and even horses to receive a blessing in the name of the saint who cared so deeply for creation.

In the centuries since Francis, poets and other writers have written about our spiritual connection to the world God made. "Nature has some perfections to show that she is the image of God," said seventeenth-century French thinker Blaise Pascal. And Elizabeth Fry, an eighteenth-century English Quaker, wrote these words after attending a worship service: "After the meeting my heart felt really light and as I walked home by starlight, I looked through nature up to nature's God."

————

Father, what a glorious world you have created. Help me to be more aware of your fingerprints throughout all of creation.

8

A Love Renewed

For God so loved the world that he gave his one and only Son, that whoever believes in him shall not perish but have eternal life.

John 3:16

I GOT the call at 3:00 A.M. My daughter was taking her one-year-old son, Justin, to the emergency room. His raging fever had turned to hysteria, and he was screaming uncontrollably.

As I raced to the hospital, my drowsy mind filled with fearful thoughts of dreaded childhood diseases. I had regularly confronted such fears while raising my own children, and now I did so again with the first of my grandchildren. My love and concern for this little guy was so intense that I couldn't imagine my feelings could be any stronger.

I finally pulled into the hospital parking lot and dashed inside. There stood my daughter, Justin draped over her shoulder like a worn-out rag doll.

He saw me and reached out for me. I lifted him onto my own shoulder. The smell of fever and heat from his little body brought tears to my eyes.

Antibiotics soothed Justin's infected ears and restored calm to a frazzled family, but as I drove back home, I thought about the pain involved in loving anyone deeply. I would gladly suffer for Justin, but would I allow him to suffer for anyone else? Never! My love for him is so great that I could never allow this.

As the streetlights sped by my window in the morning darkness, the words of John 3:16 came to mind: "For God so loved the world that he gave his one and only son. . . ."

These are the words children learn in their earliest Sunday school lessons. These are the words sin-sick sinners hear at Billy Graham crusades. These are the words I myself have turned to for comfort so many times.

Millions of Christians can recite these words from memory, but has such familiarity bred indifference? Have we grown complacent about God's revolutionary good news?

"For God so loved the world" is more than six words in a book. It's an earthquake shaking our foundations. It's a reminder that God loves us more than I love my grandson.

Such love is incomprehensible. It's like a fish trying to grasp the concept of water. But if we are willing to take an occasional break from life's incessant busyness, words grown dull with familiarity can become living truths once again.

For me, it was an early morning drive to the hospital that renewed my spiritual passion. For you, perhaps something less dismaying can shed new light on old truths.

―――――――

Thank you, God, for loving this world and everyone in it, including me. I don't always understand such love, but help me to experience it in my life.

9

Made in God's Image

Then God said, "Let us make man in our image. . . ."
. . . So God created man in his own image,
in the image of God he created him;
male and female he created them.

Genesis 1:26–27

OUR world is full of dozens of high-tech gadgets that are supposed to simplify our hectic lives.

It's clear that cars are faster than chariots, and that microwave ovens cook more quickly than traditional ovens. But have you ever tried to debug your computer when it goes haywire? Or have you ever tried to program your videocassette recorder to tape one of your favorite TV programs while you're out of the house?

If you're like me, you've had more than your share of frustrating moments with machines and appliances that don't respond to foot stomping, grumbling, or frantic searches through owners' manuals full of indecipherable mumbo jumbo.

One way to understand the purpose of the Bible is to see it as a divinely inspired owner's manual for operation and maintenance of human life. And while parts of the Bible are complex and hard to understand, passages like this one in Genesis are both straightforward and powerful.

Though the passage contains only thirty-two words, it delivers three important lessons: First, God is not a *me* but an *us*. Our God is a union consisting of three persons: heavenly Father, Holy Spirit, and only begotten Son. For centuries theologians have called this concept the Trinity or the Godhead.

Second, when God created humanity he made us in his own image. As the first two chapters of Genesis show, God created everything that exists, and nothing exists that he did not create. He gave all of these things his loving attention, but when it came to creating humanity, the Bible tells us that this was a special occasion. When God created us, he gave birth to something truly unique.

So what does it mean when the Bible says God created us in his image? For one thing, it means that humans are creative. Some of us use our God-given creativity to make music, design Web pages, write love poems, or arrange flowers for others to see. Though some may forget it, this ability to create comes directly from God.

Third, God created humans in two distinct types: male and female. Although men and women are different, they are alike in many essential ways. In addition, God loves both sexes equally. There's no gender superiority in creation.

Owner's manuals may not help us understand how to work our VCRs, but God's owner's manual will help us understand who we are and how God intends us to live.

———

God, life often seems hectic and complex, and technology seems to make things even crazier. But I thank you for creating men and women as you did and for caring about us as much as you do.

10

Vanishing Fears

I am not ashamed of the gospel, because it is the power of God for the salvation of everyone who believes: first for the Jew, then for the Gentile.

Romans 1:16

I CAN'T do this," I whispered to the pastor leading the teams of people going out to share the gospel.

"Of course you can," he said in a matter-of-fact way.

He doesn't get it, I thought. *He doesn't understand that I am really afraid to knock on the doors of perfect strangers and ask them about God.*

I had been in a witnessing program at my church for several months and had overcome my initial fear of calling on church visitors. These people were predisposed to talk about spiritual things. They had attended a worship service and signed a visitor's card.

But now we were to go out and knock on doors in apartment buildings near the church and ask the residents to answer some questions about their belief in God.

"It isn't you doing this anyway," the pastor said to me. "You know it is the power of God in you."

It sure didn't feel like the power of God was anywhere near me as

I headed out the door with two visiting pastors. They were attending a training program at our church to see how laypeople could learn to share effectively their faith and lead others to Christ.

I didn't reveal my misgivings to them but offered up a fervent, silent prayer for the courage I really couldn't feel.

I agreed with Paul in Romans 1:16 when he said that he was not ashamed of the gospel. I could also affirm that the gospel has the power to bring salvation to those who believe it. But it seemed impossible that I could express God's power in any meaningful way.

No one answered our knocking at the first few doors, but then a middle-aged woman invited us in. She told us that she had attended church all of her life, so I was certain that we would have nothing new to share.

As I started to talk with her about her understanding of who Jesus is and what he did, my fear began to disappear. She was interested and eager to talk about a new faith that wasn't based on her good deeds in order to please God.

An hour or so later she prayed and invited Jesus into her life. All of us—the woman, the two pastors, and I—were excited to be present when the power of the gospel transformed the thinking of this dear lady.

On another occasion, I was part of a group of Christians who went out on the beaches of Ft. Lauderdale to talk to college kids from all over the United States who had descended on south Florida for spring break. I began talking with one young man who listened to me for a few minutes and then said, "You couldn't possibly understand why I hate God."

"Try me," I responded.

He went on to tell me that his fiancée was killed the previous Christmas when a motorist drove up on a curb and ran over her.

It was amazing to me as I listened to him to think that, of all the people on the beach, God had led me to this young man. I went on to tell him how my own husband had been killed just ten days before Christmas two years before.

He was very interested in how I could love God in spite of what happened. When we parted ways, he said he was willing to think more about God and pray that God would change him.

I witnessed so many encounters similar to these over the years where people's hearts and minds were changed.

And it was especially obvious to me that the power came from God and not any persuasive words from me. When God is at work, information one has learned in a classroom becomes infused with supernatural meaning. And *anyone* can be God's tool of salvation!

———

Father, thank you that you choose to use us as vessels through which your Holy Spirit works.

11

Innocence in God's Garden

The man and his wife were both naked, and they felt no shame.

Genesis 2:25

Bᴿɪᴛɪꜱʜ novelist and essayist C. S. Lewis once described the problem of runaway sexual appetites in his uniquely witty style:

Now suppose you came to a country where you could fill a theater by simply bringing a covered plate on to the stage and then slowly lifting the cover so as to let everyone see, just before the lights went out, that it contained a mutton chop or a bit of bacon, would you not think that in that country something had gone wrong with the appetite for food? And would not anyone who had grown up in a different world think there was something equally queer about the state of the sex instinct among us?[1]

When God created Adam and Eve, he lavished special care on human sexuality. Sex was to be the means by which humans reproduced—just as in the animal kingdom. But with humans, whom God created uniquely in his own image, there was more to sex than breeding.

In the divine drama, God designed sex as a means for a man and a woman to experience deeper intimacy with each other than would be possible in any other way. That's why Adam and Eve were naked but unashamed.

Shame came later. By C. S. Lewis's day, sex had become popular in stage shows, magazines, and movies. Today, sexually explicit material is available on video, DVD, and the Internet, where people need only a computer, a modem, and a phone line to view images that would have been illegal or not readily available only a decade or two ago.

Are we better today in our so-called sexually liberated age than earlier generations of men and women? Lewis wouldn't think so. Though God gave us our appetites, we must control them.

Without control, we become enslaved by our appetites. People enslaved by food are guilty of the biblical sin of gluttony and reap the consequences of obesity and health problems. Those who are enslaved by sex are guilty of lust and find themselves among a growing number of sex addicts.

Lewis said: There is a story about a schoolboy who was asked what he thought God was like. He replied that, as far as he could make out, God was "the sort of person who is always snooping round to see if anyone is enjoying himself and then trying to stop it."[2]

That's not it at all. God's no heavenly killjoy. He wants us to know the innocence and intimacy Adam and Eve knew in the Garden of Eden. He desires for us to know what it means to be naked and unashamed.

———

Father, thank you for the gift of sex. Help me to use it wisely.

12

The Benefit of Trials

Consider it pure joy, my brothers, whenever you face trials of many kinds.

James 1:2

RON and Cathy, dear friends of my daughter and her husband, just welcomed their fourth child into their family. Colton was born about four weeks early, but all seemed well. For a while, that is.

A few hours after he was born, the trial began. A nurse expressed concern that Colton might have Down's syndrome and the doctor ordered tests to confirm or deny her suspicions. For three days, differing opinions from doctors and nurses held Ron and Cathy in the sway of emotions between fear and hope.

When the results came in, their dread became reality. Their precious new baby did have Down's.

"Consider it pure joy" seems a cruel command in the face of such pain. What can it mean?

I don't think that God expects us to *feel* joyful when difficulties occur. Our natural and automatic response to the pain of trials is to feel sad or shocked, fearful, confused, disappointed, or a combination of these emotions.

But after some time has passed and understanding of the challenges we face has sunk in, then we may be able to step back and view our situation from God's perspective. Pain is still present, and we still entreat God to intervene in ways that make life right again. But we are willing to reflect on what James meant when he began his letter with this command.

One of the most comforting truths about our relationship with God is that he is with us. We do not face our trials alone but walk with the Creator of the universe, who can supernaturally change our perspective. Awareness of his presence can begin to move us from fear to godly peace.

Once we are aware of his presence, we find our belief strengthened. We do not demand that our circumstances change, but we believe that God's love will infuse our sadness. God's touch will soften the blow we have endured and move us from questioning *Why?* to asking *How?*

Little Colton is six months old now and each day brings new challenges mixed with hopeful progress. Ron and Cathy explain their feelings this way:

"When we were given Colton's diagnosis, of course we went through the gamut of negative emotions: anger, grief, sadness, depression, fear, resentment, disbelief, and helplessness. We cried out to God. 'Lord we love you, how can you do this to our son?' We accused God of being mean and cruel.

"But through all of our tears, God was faithful to whisper to us in his still, small voice. 'I did this that I might be glorified.' His Holy Spirit soon redirected our grief into faith. Faith that He was in control. Faith that He loved Colton even more than we did. Faith that He can and indeed would heal our son."

I know that many tears still fall and many tough times lie ahead for this family, but I know also that their faith prevails. They have had a little time to adjust to the shock of this baby's condition and have moved from panic to awareness of God's goodness. They are learning how God wants them to live instead of focusing on why this happened.

Friends and pastors visit, people offer prayers, God's Spirit weaves mysteriously within Ron and Cathy and the family of faith who surround them. And joy surfaces.

————

Father, we are so grateful that your Spirit invades our lives and touches our most painful emotions with your peace. Help us to be receptive to your transforming presence.

13

The Doorway to the Heart

You have heard that it was said, "Do not commit adultery." But I tell you that anyone who looks at a woman lustfully has already committed adultery with her in his heart.

Matthew 5:27–28

PERHAPS one of God's most amazing creations is the human mind. And this verse vividly declares how vulnerable the mind can be to temptations that turn its power in ungodly directions. What a person can imagine can impact his or her heart.

Our culture is full of lustful ploys that taunt and tease. Modest dress is an idea that seems provincial in a day and age when exposing a lot of skin is the norm. "Low-cut" and "short" describe many of the clothing options for women of all ages.

Why would Jesus consider lusting after a sexy woman on television or relishing a long look at an attractive woman walking down the street adultery in the heart? I think it is because the mind, the heart and the soul are connected. What we think impacts how we feel and that impacts how we act. A mere glance can turn the wonder of sex as God intended it into a damaging force if the person glancing isn't aware of the mind's power. People with good intentions can find themselves in the middle of illicit relationships and wonder how they got there.

How did something God wonderfully created become an instrument of pain, confusion, disappointment, and distrust? People don't generally fall into sexually immoral situations easily. There is a process that begins in the mind and ends in physical entanglement. The first part of that process is mental. When a man looks lustfully at a woman he has a choice to make. Will he entertain that thought and keep that image in his mind, or will he replace it with a pure thought? If the lustful thought lingers, it can soon turn into an emotional attachment. Thoughts can become feelings that have a powerful pull on him. He can become emotionally dependent on the woman without any physical touch.

And if the emotions grow, the man may finally express them to the woman. If she is vulnerable and chooses unwisely, a relationship may develop that leads to physical adultery, with all its damage, pain, and broken trust.

In the passage from Matthew, we can also see Jesus making it clear that he did not come to earth to do away with God's law. If anything, he emphasized God's law in new and even more demanding ways. When Jesus told his disciples that there was more to lust than sexual behavior, he wasn't downplaying the sinful destructiveness of adultery. Rather, he was showing that if we focus on sin when it has already been committed, we are starting too late.

Each of the acts prohibited in the Ten Commandments (Exodus 20) starts with an offense of the heart. Idolatry begins with a lack of faith in God and a desire to turn elsewhere for supernatural help. Murder begins with anger. Robbery begins with greed and a jealousy for other people's possessions.

Jesus isn't telling us to ignore sin. What he's trying to do is get us to look within our hearts, examine our souls, and be sensitive to the roots of sinful attitudes that, if permitted to grow unhindered, will undoubtedly blossom into future sinful acts.

He's also trying to challenge us to discipline our minds so that they think godly thoughts. For it is with our thoughts that we often sow the seeds of future sins.

————

Father, help me to clean out the roots of sin before they grow into sinful acts.

14

Life Is a Learning Adventure

Now we see but a poor reflection as in a mirror; then we shall see face to face. Now I know in part; then I shall know fully, even as I am fully known.

1 Corinthians 13:12

A YOUNG woman asked me to help her decide if she or her husband was right about an issue. Both were sure that God had told them the answer to their dilemma, but their "words from God" were different.

We talked and concluded that it is often difficult to be really clear about what God is saying. The way we see God is obscured, in part, because he doesn't reveal all of himself to us this side of heaven.

The mirror 1 Corinthians 13:12 mentions would have been made of a metal, probably bronze. The people of New Testament times polished the metal until they could see their reflections, but even then they would have been blurry and discolored.

God tells us that we see him with the same lack of clarity that using such a mirror would produce. We are limited in our knowledge of him.

This reminds me of the early years of my marriage to Steve. We met, fell in love, spent lots of time together, and married after being pretty sure we knew each other very well.

As our day-to-day life unfolded, though, I was so often surprised at Steve's reactions, responses, ideas. I'm sure he felt the same way. We had seen each other as a poor reflection in a polished metal mirror.

Our marriage is not unusual. Couples learn new and wonderful (sometimes, not so wonderful) things about their mates for many years as they grow together. And as they learn, they can enjoy each other more and more. Even now some of the new things we discover about each other after thirteen years of marriage still surprise us. This continual revelation makes life an adventure.

Our adventure with God through the years reveals more and more about him also. We grow closer to him and understand more of his Word. And then, when he comes back we will experience knowing him and being fully known. We will see God face-to-face. How amazing to contemplate that God is willing to reveal all of himself to us.

Sometimes when he seems distant or his Word seems hard to understand, it may be helpful to look with a long view to the time when the reflection of God that we see now will be crystal clear. Any confusion we have about who is hearing him more accurately will be gone.

In the meantime, we do the best we can to reason together, pray, seek counsel, and make decisions with open hearts toward one another—rather than debating who is right and who is wrong!

———

Father, we look forward to the day when we will be fully in your presence. Thank you for glimpses now that give us a taste of the future.

15

Grace or Guilt?

For the LORD your God is a consuming fire, a jealous God. . . . For the LORD your God is a merciful God; he will not abandon or destroy you or forget the covenant with your forefathers, which he confirmed to them by oath.

Deuteronomy 4:24, 31

How do you picture God? Loving or punishing? Forgiving or judgmental?

Mark Twain was a leading humorist of his day, but he also had his dark, pessimistic side. In one of his angry essays on religion, Twain described the biblical God as a malevolent monster who made people blind by poking out their eyes, made people deformed by making one leg shorter than the other, and then laughed about all the cruel hardships he had inflicted.

Painters have also added their unique visions to our perceptions of God. Michelangelo's *The Creation of Man*, a huge fresco that adorns the ceiling of Rome's Sistine Chapel, shows God as a bearded, muscular elderly man who, surrounded by angels, extends his hand toward a reclining nude Adam.

Centuries later, William Blake's work *The Ancient of Days* shows

God as a bearded, muscular young man who uses an engineering device to measure the world he is making.

From what did your image of God come?

If your earthly father was warm and loving, that may help you have a positive image of God. But for people who have suffered through parental abuse, picturing God as a loving heavenly father can often be difficult.

None of us will ever have a complete picture of God until we get to heaven. Even Moses, who had a direct encounter with God, never saw the Creator in all his glory.

In this life, the best way for us to gain an accurate picture of God is by studying the clues the Bible provides for us. And as the two verses in Deuteronomy show, this process isn't always easy.

In the Book of Deuteronomy, Moses knew that God was so angry at him for his disobedience that he would not permit Moses to go with the Israelites to the promised land (Num. 20:1–13). Before Moses left the people he had led for four decades, he once again explained the laws of God to them. It was during this instruction that he called God both "a consuming fire" and "a merciful God."

How could both of these things be true? A review of the preceding books of the Bible repeatedly answers this question. When God's people turned against him and his commands, his anger and judgment were fierce. But when his people recognized the errors of their ways, repented, and returned to God in sincerity and submission, his grace and forgiveness knew no limits.

It's the same for us today. It's not God who is changing, it's us.

————

God, you are both a consuming fire and a merciful father. Help me live my life in such a way that it's your mercy I see.

16

A Big Command from a Small Place

Therefore go and make disciples of all nations, baptizing them in the name of the Father and of the Son and of the Holy Spirit.

Matthew 28:19

STEVE and I were able to visit Israel before an eruption of violence almost stopped tourism to this fascinating country. In ten days we traveled the length and breadth of that historic region, visiting most of the places where Jesus had lived and ministered.

We recalled Old Testament stories of David and his time in the Judean Desert as he fled from Saul, and we drove by Jericho near the land the Israelites claimed when they crossed the Jordan after wandering in the desert for forty years.

Jesus spoke the famous command of Matthew 28:19, which is known as the Great Commission, on a mountain in Galilee. The Sea of Galilee is really a lake and the mountains surrounding it seem like large hills to this Colorado resident. But the surprising size didn't diminish the impact of walking where Jesus walked.

The hillside was grass-covered and lush. Tropical bushes and flowers bloomed and the Sea of Galilee sparkled in the sunshine at the base of the hill. While there I reflected that when Jesus spoke the words of the Great Commission in this same spot or a similar one nearby, he spoke only to the remaining eleven disciples.

I've often wondered if they could even begin to grasp the power he was bestowing on them to carry out this task. Their own world was small.

Israel today is only 256 miles north to south and 81 miles east to west, with a 143-mile coastline. The disciples would have been primarily in the regions where Jesus ministered, and it wasn't until after the persecution of the church (Acts 8) that other believers scattered from the communities in Israel where they lived.

As Steve and I traveled around in our tour bus I certainly understood that Jesus and the disciples had covered ground on foot. But in light of the words of the Great Commission I was, and am, still amazed at the small number of people and the relatively puny geographic size of their country. The Roman Empire completely dwarfed them, and yet they became the world's most populous religion.

These men had none of the trappings of power that would be associated with world movements; no numbers, no wealth, no political influence, no prestige, no troops. All they had was their firsthand witness to the miracle of God incarnate and the promise of the Holy Spirit to come and reside in each of them.

The disciples of ancient Israel received this verse and obeyed. And now we are a part of their heritage.

———

Father, thank you for the obedience of those eleven men who sat with Jesus on a hillside in Galilee. We marvel at what is still unfolding as a result of their faith. Help us to believe that even we can impact the world for Christ.

17

Passing the Buck

The man said, "The woman you put here with me—she gave me some
fruit from the tree, and I ate it."
Then the LORD God said to the woman, "What is this you have done?"
The woman said, "The serpent deceived me, and I ate."

Genesis 3:12–13

ONE warm spring day—when you would have rather been anywhere than in math class—your teacher looked you straight
in the eyes and asked you where your assignment was.

You squirmed uncomfortably in your seat, ransacking your mental library for a plausible alibi, until you came up with the following
excuse: "My dog ate it."

You didn't have a dog. And even more important, you didn't have
a finished assignment for an imaginary canine companion to consume.

Still, you offered up your lame excuse. And as you did so, you
prayed to whatever God you could imagine that your teacher would
not hear your heart beating like a bass drum or see the rivers of
sweat rolling down your face.

"Well," she said, "I expect you to do the assignment over and
bring it in with you tomorrow."

Twenty-five years later you found yourself on the hot seat again, only this time it was your boss demanding to see the quarterly sales report for the next day's meeting. For a split second you considered resurrecting the dog excuse but thought better of it.

"I'm just waiting for a final number from our Hong Kong office," you said, hoping your boss would believe you this time.

U.S. President Harry Truman had a handwritten sign on his desk that read: "The buck stops here." But for many of us, passing the buck is more our style.

After all, passing the buck is a popular human pastime that traces its origins to the dawn of human history. Adam, the first man God created, was also the first man to avoid taking responsibility for his failures.

After God created the earth, he told Adam and Eve not to eat the fruit from the tree in the middle of the garden. "You must not touch it, or you will die," said God (Gen. 2:17).

But the serpent tricked Eve into eating. Then Eve persuaded Adam to eat. This was the beginning of sin—a tragedy theologians call the fall of humanity.

When God asked Adam and Eve what had happened, they tried to fool the Creator of the cosmos with a flimsy con job.

"Eve gave it to me," said Adam.

"The serpent deceived me," said Eve.

Things might be much different today if Adam had said, "God, I confess. I messed up. I'm sorry."

He didn't, and he paid the price. So do we.

God, help me own up to my mistakes and apologize to those I may have hurt. Help me take responsibility for my sin instead of endlessly passing the buck.

18

Equal in God's Sight

There is neither Jew nor Greek, slave nor free, male nor female, for you are all one in Christ Jesus.

Galatians 3:28

THE apostle Paul had a problem in the province of Galatia. The Jewish Christians in that area held tightly to many of the Old Testament laws and tried to impose them on converts to Christianity. They were especially concerned that all men be circumcised. Some of the Galatian legalists argued that Paul was not really an apostle and was using his teachings on grace and freedom to help persuade nonbelievers to convert.

In his letter to the Galatians Paul wrote to free followers of the gospel from the bonds of legalism. Galatians 3:28 is a strong statement for equality and the laying down of comparisons. It places all believers on level ground before Christ based on their belief in him and not on any works they have done or will do. Christ loves and receives them just as they are, without the need to perform in order to win his approval.

How wonderful it must have been for the early Christians who were Greeks, slaves, or women to hear this teaching in Galatians.

What about us today? Do we claim that all are saved by faith alone but then regard people based on their performance or their status in society? Do we even damage ourselves with comparisons to other Christians whom we view as more accomplished or more significant than we feel we are? Do we wonder if Christ really thinks as well of us as he does of others?

Our culture thrives on comparisons. Advertisements—designed to appeal to our desire to shine above everyone else, to win, to get the guy or girl who is the most popular, to be the envy of everyone we pass—continually bombard us.

But the quest for this kind of recognition is endless. There is always someone else who is prettier, richer, more talented. Or in the Christian world, there are always people who work harder, give more, do more.

Can it really be that Christ loves us equally, saves us totally by his grace, frees us to be who God created us to be and not a "better" version of someone else?

Paul declared that this grace is real and is ours. When we accept this blessing, we are not only free to stop comparing ourselves unfavorably to others, but we are also free to value them for who they are. Our differences don't disappear but they no longer separate us.

In Paul's day it meant that the circumcised Jewish believer and the uncircumcised Greek believer were both saved if they believed in Christ and he loved them, regardless of this physical difference.

A slave could accept Christ and embrace the spiritual freedom that salvation brings, even if he remained a slave.

That same equality is ours today.

———

Father, help us to see ourselves and each other as you do.

19

You're Not As Smart As You Think

Woe to those who are wise in their own eyes
and clever in their own sight.

Isaiah 5:21

I F you read the sermons of Old Testament prophets such as Isaiah, Jeremiah, and Daniel, you'll find plenty of verses that begin with that scary three-letter word: woe.

A psychotherapist might say that these prophets suffered from some kind of psychosis, depression, or dissociative disorder. But the Bible has a different explanation for their often hard-edged pronouncements. God called prophets to convey his messages to the world. And some of these messages indicated God's frustration with the ways humans repeatedly mess up their own lives.

One of the human failings that shows up throughout the messages of Isaiah and the other prophets is the sin of intellectual pride. God doesn't have any problems with people being smart. After all, to begin with, it was God who created brains. What does trouble God is when the people he created think they're so smart they can live life without any help from him. If this scenario sounds familiar, that's because it's part of a recurring pattern.

In the Garden of Eden, Adam and Eve decided that they could disobey God's commands about not eating the fruit of one particular tree. Through their act of intellectual pride, humanity's first couple introduced sin to the entire race.

Even earlier, pride had caused the downfall of an angelic being who declared: "I will ascend to heaven; / I will raise my throne above the stars of God" (Isa. 14:13). God banished this prideful archangel from heaven. Today, he is known as Satan.

Pride—and its close relative, rebellion—appears frequently in the pages of Scripture. It was there when the ancestors of Noah built the Tower of Babel. It was there when the Israelites created a golden calf and worshiped it instead of God. It was there when David had an illicit affair with Bathsheba and killed her loving husband to hide his shame. And it was there when a disciple named Judas took thirty pieces of silver to snitch on Jesus.

It's not that God wants people to be stupid. In the early 1900s, a famous evangelist named Billy Sunday said: "I don't know any more about theology than a jackrabbit knows about Ping-Pong, but I'm on my way to glory!" Actually God is fine with learning, scholarship, and intelligence. It's just when we think we're smart enough to go it alone that we cross the line and experience woe.

———

Father, thank you for giving me an amazing mind, and for the grace to know I'm not as smart as I think.

20

A Gentle Evangelist

*But in your hearts set apart Christ as Lord. Always be prepared to give
an answer to everyone who asks you to give the reason for the hope that
you have. But do this with gentleness and respect.*

1 Peter 3:15

For a number of years I was a rather zealous evangelist. I actively
shared my faith and participated in a weekly witnessing program
at my church.

Sometimes I remember those days with heartfelt grief. Certainly a
lot of people prayed to accept Jesus with me, but my aggressiveness
put off a number of others. I felt so sure of my message, but I often
shared without sensitivity. I grieve over the ones who didn't understand about Jesus because my bravado got in the way.

I used to talk a lot about not hiding our lights under bushels
(Matt. 5:15), but I was guilty of presenting the loving light of Jesus
in a way more akin to blazing neon.

Many Christians are in the spotlight today expressing their opinions on a wide range of issues: abortion, homosexuality, family val-

ues, politics. Is the light that others see focused on Jesus and his gift of salvation or on other issues?

I remember being at a political meeting several years ago where non-Christians expressed great concern about the views of Christians. It made me sad that no one mentioned the God we serve or his Son. They understood little about the Jesus we follow.

This verse from 1 Peter contains three primary points: set apart Christ as Lord; always be prepared to give an answer; and do this with gentleness and respect. In the past, I focused on the second point.

But oh, the power of a word spoken with the sensitivity of the Savior. Jesus was no weakling who wimped out if someone opposed him or argued with him. But he was gentle (Matt. 21:5), even when tried and wrongly convicted. On the cross he uttered, "Father, forgive them, for they do not know what they are doing" (Luke 23:34).

I think the ability to be gentle and respectful to people who do not yet know Jesus comes from the command at the beginning of this verse: "But in your hearts set apart Christ as Lord." With Christ as Lord of our hearts we comprehend our own fallenness and the graciousness of Jesus to have died for us. We are able to look at others with compassion instead of condemnation, because we know that we are just as they are: guilty but forgiven.

Jesus gives us the power to speak in ways that convey his love and woos doubters to him. It is only after people feel loved that they are able to hear words of conviction that lead to change.

And the power of words spoken with tenderness and respect helps to usher listeners in the forgiving presence of the Savior.

————

Father, thank you for calling us to you with the gentleness of Jesus.

21

Roots of Righteousness

Blessed is the man
who does not walk in the counsel
of the wicked
or stand in the way of sinners
or sit in the seat of mockers.
But his delight is in the law of the LORD,
and on his law he meditates day and night.

Psalm 1:1–2

THEY weren't preachers or priests. In fact, they weren't official representatives of any particular religious tradition or group. But when four famous young musicians named John, Paul, George, and Ringo traveled to India to study something called transcendental meditation with a guru named Maharishi Mahesh Yogi, people knew the world was undergoing a spiritual revolution.

Ever since the 1960s, a time of growing popularity for centuries-old Eastern religions and newfangled New Age cults, many people have assumed that meditation is a non-Christian practice. But as this psalm shows, God has been encouraging his followers to meditate on his Word for millennia.

There are 150 Psalms, which are poems designed to be sung with musical accompaniment. The idea of meditating upon God and his Word actually appears throughout the Psalms, and through much of the rest of the Bible.

Much of the time, many of us are going in a dozen different directions at once. Our hearts are torn, our minds are divided, and our prayers are fragmented and superficial. Meditation helps us go beneath the surface of our jumbled, overactive minds and tap into the richer veins of God's love and mercy.

Many people find that silence and solitude make it easier to meditate. Finding silence in the twenty-first-century world isn't always easy, but it helps if you can turn off the TV for a few moments. Solitude can be equally elusive at times, but some people find that taking a brief walk in a park gives them a few moments of the precious isolation they need. (The fact that the backdrop is God's beautiful creation doesn't hurt either.)

God wants you to meditate on him, but that doesn't mean you have to go live in a monastery. Here's how Thomas Merton, one of the twentieth century's most famous monks put it: "Not all men are called to be hermits, but all men need enough silence and solitude in their lives to enable the deep inner voice of their own true self to be heard at least occasionally."

Meditation is a God-ordained way for doing this. And if we practice it regularly, we will discover the deeper roots of God's righteousness.

Father, help me slow down enough to be alone with you and listen to what you have to tell me.

22

Better Than a Marathon

For physical training is of some value, but godliness has value for all things, holding promise for both the present life and the life to come.

1 Timothy 4:8

MANY First World countries are in a bit of a fitness frenzy. Exercise programs on television abound from the wee hours of the early morning until the midafternoon. Fitness clubs of many varying types dot the landscapes of most cities and towns. And books and videos on diets and workouts reside on numerous shelves in stores and appear on computer screens linked to many sites.

One of the motivations behind these physical pursuits is to beat the aging process. Certainly an improved quality of life is one benefit to working out, but many fitness programs play on our desire to live longer. We are told that we can add years to our lives with faithful regimens of exercise, and studies do seem to show enhanced and longer years for the physically active.

Exercise has power.

This verse from 1 Timothy tells us that holiness is of even greater value. It tells us that the power of godliness impacts "all things." Perhaps the parallel between physical fitness and righteousness holds true when it comes to the working of muscles to maintain a desired state.

A physically fit person will lose his lean form if he neglects exercise. He may be in tip-top shape one day but find his muscles turning to flab if he goes from playing football to watching it on television.

Spiritual fitness is subject to the same kind of buildup or deterioration. No matter how mature we may be, we need to practice the disciplines of the faith that build spiritual muscle. Prayer, Bible reading, meditation, worship, and fellowship are some of the ways that we gain and maintain spiritual health.

This verse in 1 Timothy tells us that godliness pays off in big ways, even bigger than the physical benefits of exercise.

Perhaps the most obvious benefit is that we grow closer to God. By being with him and reading his Word, we enlarge our wisdom. That, in turn, leads to making better choices in all areas of our lives.

Our thinking becomes transformed as we grow spiritually. We see life from God's perspective and not through the lens of ungodliness.

We are able to resist temptation because our discipline in being obedient to God is fine-tuned. And so we don't suffer the consequences of falling to the wiles of the tempter.

Most of all, we become more like Jesus. We reflect his light in a dark world and touch others with the power of his love—truly the healthiest thing we can do.

———

Father, help us to work on both our physical bodies and our spiritual souls.

23

Our Way to God

❦

I am the way and the truth and the life. No one comes to the Father except through me.

John 14:6

WE need always balance the exhilarating good news of Christianity with the harsh realities of its strict limits and urgent responsibilities.

Jesus came to earth to free us from the bondage of sin, but he also commanded us to "go and sin no more." Salvation introduces us to a new life in Christ, but this life also requires that we pick up our cross and follow Christ in a life of service.

Likewise, this passage from John is a good news/bad news proposition. The good news is that Jesus is "the way and the truth and the life." As a result, humanity's long and often fruitless search for fulfillment and meaning finds its answer in Christ, who shows us in his life and his words all the incredible riches that God has for us.

On the other hand, if Christ is the way, those who decide to go another way lose out. "No one comes to the Father except through me," he said, indicating that all other religious traditions and spiritual paths are dead ends.

How could the God who loves the world not save all the people of the world? Theologians have wrestled with this question for centuries.

Some have described salvation as a big party. The party is open to anyone who cares to come, and colorful invitations have been sent personally to everyone on earth. When it comes time for the party to be held, millions upon millions of people will turn out and have a wonderful time.

But not everyone will show up that day. Some people will get the invitation but throw it on a stack of mail and never get around to responding.

Others intend to come to the party, but various problems will prevent them. In one case, someone's car might break down along the way. In another case, a family illness or emergency might take attention away from the party. In more than a few cases, people will simply oversleep or forget all about it.

If you've ever thrown a party, you've probably heard your share of reasons for why someone didn't show up. But you didn't hassle those who had other things to do. It's a free world, and unless they had promised to bring the sodas or chips, they were free to stay home if they wanted.

The same goes for the big, glorious party God has planned for us in heaven. He's been spending an eternity getting things ready. He even sent his only Son to deliver the invitations.

Who knows who will be at God's grand party when that day arrives? At least we know he tried to invite us all. It's up to us to exchange bad news for good.

————

Father, I thank you that I have been able to hear and respond to your words of life. Help me invite others to your heavenly party.

24

Faith Takes Practice

I know what it is to be in need, and I know what it is to have plenty. I have learned the secret of being content in any and every situation, whether well fed or hungry, whether living in plenty or in want.

Philippians 4:12

THIS verse is a familiar one for me. I have often read it while in the midst of a trial and tried to claim it as my own. Unfortunately, there have been many times when contentment has eluded me and worry has resided in its place.

There are two words that stand out when I try to unravel how to experience this kind of contentment: *secret* and *learned*.

Paul revealed what his secret was in Philippians 4:13 when he wrote, "I can do everything through him who gives me strength."

I know Jesus, have accepted him, and seek to follow him in my daily life. So why does contentment sometimes seem so difficult to grasp? I think that I rely on myself more than on God. When I try to make life work well and don't succeed, I continue to wrestle with solving my dilemma on my own.

Oh, I pray and read my Bible. I say that I believe God is in control of everything, but I live as if I am in control. Instead of doing what I can and leaving the rest to God, I worry and manipulate to change circumstances. I miss the secret of contentment by being busy at fixing instead of abiding and resting in relationship with Jesus.

This is such a difficult thing to do because it seems passive, even irresponsible. I know intellectually that I experience his power when I am weak (2 Cor. 12:9–10), but I often short-circuit that power with my own efforts.

Paul's secret was to let God be God in his life. It was to trust in Christ to the extent that he fretted not when he was in jail or shipwrecked.

The other word that stands out to me is *learned*. So often when reading Scripture, I expect to be able to immediately apply what I have read. The word *learned* tells me that Paul didn't experience this contentment right away either.

In Romans 7:21–25 Paul confessed,

So I find this law at work: When I want to do good, evil is right there with me. For in my inner being I delight in God's law; but I see another law at work in the members of my body, waging war against the law of my mind and making me a prisoner of the law of sin at work within my members. What a wretched man I am! Who will rescue me from this body of death? Thanks be to God— through Jesus Christ our Lord!

We, like Paul, persevere in our learning to be content. The secret is in relationship with Jesus, the learning comes with practice.

———

Father, thank you that you are a patient God.

25

Walking the Ancient Path

This is what the LORD *says:*
"Stand at the crossroads and look;
ask for the ancient paths,
ask where the good way is,
and walk in it,
and you will find rest for your souls."

Jeremiah 6:16

MANY people act as if their favorite two words were *new* and *improved.*

We seem to believe that newer is always better than older, that the way we do things today is superior to the way we did them in the past, and the way we do them tomorrow will be even better still.

It is true that some things work more efficiently now than they did before. The world's first multipurpose electronic computer was a thirty-ton monstrosity called ENIAC that consisted of some eighteen thousand vacuum tubes and miles of copper wiring. ENIAC was created in a Pennsylvania lab in 1946, and when it was turned on, the lights of Philadelphia dimmed.

By 1971, all of ENIAC's computing power could be squeezed onto a tiny silicon wafer the size of a postage stamp.

The ways we record and play music have changed, too. Few people today play 78-rpm records, 45-rpm singles, or 12-inch vinyl albums. Even cassette players using magnetic tapes are on their way out, having been replaced by digital compact discs, which can cram more than an hour's worth of music onto a platter that's less than five inches in diameter. Granted, our technology has improved over the years. But has human life made corresponding progress?

People still suffer illness and die. Medical science has prolonged our lives and devised new treatments for many common ailments, but life still has an ending and a beginning. And no science known to humanity has been able to decrease the amount of greed, anger, jealousy, or cruelty in the world.

When it comes to Christianity, churches have been evolving ever since the time that Jesus' first disciples gathered together to remember his death and resurrection. In the twentieth century, the Pentecostal Revival, the Charismatic Movement, the Jesus Movement, and the Seeker-Sensitive Megachurch Movement have reinvented the way people do church.

But behind all our efforts at improvement, God is an eternal, unchanging force who hasn't changed the basics of what it means to worship him.

Older isn't always better, but newer isn't always better either. Before you jump on the latest religion bandwagon, stop and think. Find out what has gone before and compare the new approach to the old. And if new proposals seem like shallow attempts to be hip or relevant, stay with the ancient paths that believers have walked for millennia.

God, you've been around forever. Help me to cling to the things that are truly good in your sight, and not just the things that are new.

26

He Walked in Our Shoes

For we do not have a high priest who is unable to sympathize with our weaknesses, but we have one who has been tempted in every way, just as we are—yet was without sin.

Hebrews 4:15

Before I was widowed I would look at some widows and evaluate how they grieved. Maybe one cried all the time in public and another forever talked about her loss. While feeling sympathetic, I also made judgments about issues unknown to me.

Then my own husband was killed. I was thirty-four years old with two young daughters. It was a shocking reality. I cried every day and many nights for months. But I seldom cried in public.

One Sunday morning as I was walking into church, a woman came up to me and grabbed me by the shoulders. "You must grieve!" she shouted as she shook me with an angry force.

I had no time to respond as she walked off in a huff. As I steadied myself I went on into the sanctuary and sat down, still shaking from the encounter. *What in the world made her so angry at me?* I wondered.

Several weeks later a friend of that woman's told me that my lack of public crying had some people thinking that I wasn't grieving. Some people even wondered if I felt bad at all.

I thought of all the tears I'd shed and was astounded that anyone could think I didn't grieve. But the people who were judging me were doing the same thing I had done myself before being widowed.

There is a saying that warns us not to judge others until we have walked a mile in their shoes. In fact, some of the greatest comfort I received in those early days of widowhood came from women who had been widowed themselves. They could identify with me. They understood, firsthand, how I felt.

Over the years I have been asked to meet with widows for that same reason: they want to talk to someone who has been in the same place they are. We share a pain and therefore, a deep understanding.

Jesus, the very incarnation of God, shares that same identification with all of us. He has walked in our shoes. His temptation was like our own. He suffered as we do (Heb. 2:18). The difference between his temptation and our own is that he is without sin.

He doesn't look at our weaknesses the way I used to look at grieving people. He understands and sympathizes. He comes alongside us and gives us an example of how to be tempted but not sin: feel the pain of life that can tempt us to sin in order to find relief, but choose obedience and turn from the temptation.

———

Father, we thank you that you sent us a Sympathizer in the Person of Jesus.

27

Pain That Heals

Godly sorrow brings repentance that leads to salvation and leaves no regret, but worldly sorrow brings death.

2 Corinthians 7:10

Just about everyone who has ever used a hammer has mistakenly hit his own thumb. For most of us, doing this once or twice is enough, and we take better care the next time. But pity the poor person who repeatedly hits himself with a hammer.

Paul's wise words have much to say about the emotional and spiritual pain so many of us seem to inflict on ourselves. As he saw it, there are two kinds of inner pain: the pain that leads to life and the pain that leads to death.

We all cause pain to ourselves and others. Some of us do it fairly regularly, and some of us don't even know when we're hurting someone. But regardless, there's more than enough pain to go around.

What Paul was trying to tell us is that godly sorrow is the kind of pain that causes us to take stock of our lives and change course so we don't experience it again. This kind of sorrow leads to *repentance*, a word that appears throughout the Bible and means "to turn back."

The person who hits his thumb with a hammer and says, "Ouch, that hurts," then decides to find a more productive way of driving nails has repented. He has turned back from his old practices and decided to try things a new way.

But the person who doesn't mend his ways, and instead keeps hammering away while his thumb turns into a throbbing mess, is following a course that Paul said will lead to death.

Unless you're a professional carpenter or builder, your main problem in life probably doesn't have anything to do with a hammer. Maybe it's your ego that you swing around like a blunt instrument, hitting everyone around you and causing pain.

Or it may be that your weaknesses and desires are what get you in trouble. You want to do the right thing, but you succumb to temptation, breaking the bonds of trust and love that are so important in human relationships.

Regardless of what your particular vulnerability is, Paul's words teach us an important lesson. Pain isn't the main problem we face in life, but rather it's how we're going to react to life's plentiful sorrow and suffering.

If pain and sorrow are simply small roadblocks in our path, and we decide to speed over these bumps on the way to our destination, it's likely that pain will be our constant companion in life and we won't learn its valuable lessons.

But if we receive pain as an important message from God and repent, our sorrow and frustrations can lead us to life.

Father, thank you for the powerful way pain can bring us to our senses. Use the pain I experience to lead me to life.

28

A Healing Touch

Then he said to her, "Daughter, your faith has healed you. Go in peace."

Luke 8:48

As Jesus was walking along, crowds of people swarmed around him, almost crushing him (Luke 8:42). In the crowd was a woman who had been bleeding for twelve years. No one had been able to heal her, and she had been ceremonially unclean (Lev. 15:25–30) for all that time. In the culture of Israel, a woman who was ceremonially unclean had to live separate from other people and was considered a social outcast. No one was supposed to touch her or anything that she touched.

How lonely and desperate she must have been. Somehow she had concluded if she could just touch the edge of his "cloak" she would be healed. As soon as she tapped his garment her bleeding stopped. Jesus wanted to make her healing known and asked the crowd, "Who touched me?" (Luke 8:45)

The disciples began to talk about the crowd pushing in on Jesus, but he distinguished that closeness from the touch of the woman because he felt his power go out to her. The woman came fearfully to

Jesus and said that she had brushed against his cloak and was instantly healed.

Can we even imagine how this woman felt? She had been an "outsider" through no fault of her own, suffering not only physically but also emotionally. Then she was instantly healed and the object of her faith was asking for her. She must have been overwhelmed.

Jesus then addressed her with the endearment "daughter." Nowhere else in Jesus' recorded words does this address appear. He told her and the crowd that her faith had healed her.

This story intrigues me. I wonder what I would have done had I been that woman. Would I have had enough faith in this Jesus to believe that merely touching the edge of his garment would heal me?

Even more, do I have enough faith today to believe that my relationship with Jesus is such that I can "touch" him and experience the fruit of faith?

I have, of course, heard stories of people being scolded for too little faith that results in ills going uncured. And we all know godly saints of the Lord who have died in the throes of disease.

Where is the power of this verse for us?

I think it is in the woman's faith in her particular circumstance. She was healed and perhaps even more important, she went away in peace. The power of faith results in peace, even when circumstances don't change.

When we approach Jesus in the midst of our crowded worlds and reach out to him, confident that he will respond, we experience his peace. Our faith heals our souls, if not our circumstances.

———

Father, we are slow to trust you wholeheartedly. Enlarge our belief. Heal our souls. Help us to trust you and reach out to you.

29

What God Requires

He has showed you, O man, what is good.
And what does the LORD require of you?
To act justly and to love mercy
and to walk humbly with your God.

Micah 6:8

OVER the centuries, people have developed an amazing variety of ways for worshiping God.

In Eastern Orthodox churches, incense and icons help believers make contact with the mysteries of God.

In Catholic churches, the celebration of the Mass helps believers experience the sacramental presence of Christ in their midst.

Protestants worship God with an astounding variety of methods and styles. In many Baptist churches, the emphasis is on sermons that illustrate lessons from the Word of God. In Pentecostal and charismatic congregations, the congregation gives the Holy Spirit room to work. And in many newer churches, people in blue jeans sing contemporary praise choruses that include elements of pop and rock music.

In Micah, one of the final books of the Old Testament, the people wondered what kinds of observance God required when they gathered for worship. Foremost in their minds was their concern about how to show proper repentance for their many sins.

Micah spoke for the people, asking what God demanded:

> With what shall I come before the LORD
> and bow down before the exalted God?
> Shall I come before him with burnt offerings,
> with calves a year old?
> Will the LORD be pleased with thousands of rams,
> with ten thousand rivers of oil?
> Shall I offer my firstborn for my transgression,
> the fruit of my body for the sin of my soul? (Micah 6:6–7)

But God wasn't concerned primarily with external demonstrations of reverence. Burnt offerings and ritual sacrifices weren't the things he wanted to see.

Rather, God demanded a deeper commitment. He wanted people to worship him from the depths of their hearts and live their lives in such a way that their daily actions revealed their love for God: "And what does the LORD require of you? / To act justly and to love mercy / and to walk humbly with your God."

God commanded his people to act justly: *Don't cheat your neighbor and then come to my altar to make a sacrifice. Don't exploit your workers and then come make some kind of superficial religious show.*

God also commanded his people to love mercy: *When you see someone in need, reach out in love and compassion. When someone is hopeless or weary, provide strength and courage.*

Finally, God commanded his people to worship him with humility: *Crucify your pride. Lay your ego on the altar. Come before me recognizing that I am God, and that you are not.*

People can worship God in all kinds of ways, but the principles of worship never change. God wants us to live lives of justice, mercy, and humility.

If these virtues take root in your life, God will graciously accept your worship, no matter what outward form it takes.

———

God, help me be the just and merciful servant you want me to be.

30

A Focused Life

For I resolved to know nothing while I was with you except Jesus Christ and him crucified.

1 Corinthians 2:2

PAUL wrote this letter to the believers in Corinth after hearing of problems within their community. The church was gifted (1:4–7) but immature and unspiritual (3:1–4). They suffered from divisiveness in the body, immorality, legal dealings in the pagan courts, and disrespect in participating in the Lord's Supper.

Given the environment of Corinth, Paul might have been tempted to resort to worldly arguments. It was a major city of its day. Its location on the narrow isthmus connecting the Greek mainland with the Peloponnese, the southernmost part of Greece, afforded it a dominant place in world trade. It had two harbors and was the crossroads for travelers and traders.

Corinth was also a cosmopolitan place. Its people placed high value on wisdom and were interested in the philosophies of Greek scholars. Corinth was also a religious center with at least twelve temples. One of the most famous was the temple dedicated to Aphrodite, the goddess of love.

Corinth was so widely known for its practice of sexual immorality in the name of religion (related to the worship of Aphrodite) that the practice of sexual immorality was known as "Corinthianizing." (Introduction to 1 Corinthians; the *NIV Study Bible*)

Paul understood the power of knowing Jesus to turn people from their sin, even in a city so filled with ungodliness. In 1 Corinthians 1 Paul presented his argument for this power by speaking out against the "wisdom" of men, including the Greek philosophers. Then in the opening of 1 Corinthians 2 he gave a disclaimer so that no one would think he was trying to persuade them in the same way the Greek philosophers were. "My message and my preaching were not with wise and persuasive words, but with a demonstration of the Spirit's power, so that your faith might not rest on men's wisdom, but on God's power." The truth of the crucifixion and the resurrection confounded the worldly wisdom of the age. The same is true today.

We live in an advanced society that greatly values intellect and wealth. We are inundated with persuasions to buy more, to be better than the next guy in just about anything, to discover self and indulge it.

It's tempting to talk about our faith in ways that promise the same kind of presumed satisfaction that the world offers. But Paul told us that focusing on Jesus and what he did for us is the way to penetrate minds filled with lies.

Paul's first letter to the Corinthians lifted Christ up high and taught that his wisdom had the power of the Holy Spirit behind it.

———

Father, we live in a world full of temptations not unlike those in Corinth. Help us to guard our hearts and focus on Jesus.

31

A New Command

A new command I give you: Love one another. As I have loved you, so you must love one another. By this all men will know that you are my disciples, if you love one another.

John 13:34–35

GOD gave Moses the Ten Commandments, which would be the Law for thousands of years. These commandments were simple and direct. Among other things, the people of Israel were to have no other gods; they were to avoid robbery, murder, and adultery, and they were to honor their mothers and fathers.

Even though there were only ten commandments, they were difficult to follow. Throughout the Old Testament, God's people repeatedly broke his laws and experienced the consequences of their actions.

Jesus came to earth to renew God's covenant, but this time with the entire earth. And Jesus came teaching a new commandment: "Love one another."

Although this may sound simple, it's the hardest thing to do, particularly when we understand the commitment needed to follow the second part: "As I have loved you, so you must love one another."

How did Jesus love us? By coming from heaven to save us, and dying for us on the cross. Following Jesus' new commandment to love means that we must be willing to lay down our lives for others.

So how have we done in the nearly two thousand years since Christ taught this new commandment? Not very well.

People still fight, rob, and steal, and nations still engage in wars against other nations. Even in churches, the places where one might expect that Jesus' love would remain supreme, there are political fights and turf battles that seem more petty than some of the struggles outside the church. In some churches, division over styles of music can lead to all-out "worship wars," with those who prefer traditional hymns attacking those who prefer more contemporary worship choruses. In others, disagreements about how money is raised and spent can weaken the bonds of love.

Jesus said, "By this all men will know that you are my disciples, if you love one another." If that's the case, people looking at the church may be justified in wondering if those who call themselves Christians are truly his disciples.

So what can we do now to make Christ's new command a reality in our lives? We can't erase two millennia of religious infighting and hatred overnight. But with each new day, we can begin living our lives as if love mattered.

That could involve big things. One powerful example of love was apparent when relatives of victims of the September 11, 2001, attacks on the World Trade Center forgave the terrorists who were responsible for killing nearly three thousand people.

It could involve small things, too. When you're driving your car down a busy freeway and someone pulls in front of you, can you forgive him for his rudeness and even better yet, pray for him? At church, living as if love mattered means practicing charity toward those who have different views about music or money or other potentially divisive issues and remembering that God loves all his children equally.

Jesus never said his new command would be easy to follow. But he did teach us that life wouldn't make any sense without love.

———

Father, help me love people as you have loved me. Let love overflow in me until it moves me to reach out to others.

32

We Don't Look So Good Either

But God demonstrates his own love for us in this: While we were still sinners, Christ died for us.

Romans 5:8

His name was Don and he was homeless. One of the families in our church had employed Don to do some odd jobs and asked Steve if we had any work for him. We did have some yard and outside projects that Steve hadn't gotten to, so we said yes.

I felt good about our decision, and probably a bit self-righteous. I thought, *Won't he be grateful?* At the same time my heart did hurt whenever I drove past bedraggled men (and once in a while, women) on street corners holding signs asking for a meal or a job.

So it was with mixed feelings of pride at our "goodness" and sincere sorrow for his plight, that Steve went to pick up Don at the parking lot where he slept in a run-down van. He came in the garage with Steve, and I went out to greet him.

He was really dirty. His clothes were torn and smelled of sweat and cigarettes. I shook his hand and saw the red-ringed needle marks. My smile masked my revulsion, but I went back in the house as quickly as I could.

Don worked for us on and off for several months, and I admit that I never felt comfortable around him. Steve tried to help Don improve; he let him shower at our house, Don ate with us and heard about God's love for him, and Steve worked with him until Don ended up in jail and finally left town.

Don's sins were so easy to see. He continued to make poor choices and turn down help. He was not easy to love, or even like. But God tells us in this verse that "while we were still sinners, Christ died for us."

Yes, I think to myself, *but we—my family, friends, and I—are not like Don. We are not dirty and drug-ridden. Surely we are easier to love . . . or even die for.*

But just as I am puffing myself up by comparison to one less privileged than I am, another verse comes to mind: ". . . For all have sinned and fall short of the glory of God" (Rom. 3:23).

All have sinned. All of us.

And the amazing truth of God's love is that he poured it out on us while we were still sinners. Even after accepting his Son, we still make mistakes and commit sins. And he still loves us.

Jesus went willingly to the cross for the love of people like Don and you and me. What Don displayed outwardly, we carry in our hearts. We are full of unlovely trappings, but God comes in and cleanses us. Every "Don" can be white as snow.

———

Father, thank you that our salvation is not based on how good we are but on your amazing grace.

33

Created and Called

The word of the LORD came to me, saying,
"Before I formed you in the womb I knew you,
before you were born I set you apart;
I appointed you as a prophet to the nations."

Jeremiah 1:4–5

JEREMIAH was a servant of God who lived six centuries before the time of Christ. Many call him "the weeping prophet" because of the intense, emotional nature of his prophecies of doom and judgment.

Jeremiah had served as a priest before God called him to be a prophet—a person who would tell the people what God was thinking. And like Moses centuries earlier, Jeremiah initially resisted God's call. "I do not know how to speak," he said. "I am only a child" (Jer. 1:6).

God wasn't moved by his protests. "You must go to everyone I send you to and say whatever I command you" (Jer. 1:7).

God also reassured Jeremiah that this new calling was no spur-of-the-moment thing. "Before I formed you in the womb I knew you," he said. "Before you were born I set you apart."

God calls each one of us to do things that no one else on earth can do. He calls few prophets, but he does command us to serve him in the ways we can with the years we have left.

For some, this means we will be involved in various forms of ministry such as preaching or teaching in a church, serving as a missionary, or working as an elder to guide the life of a church and its members.

Most of us, though, will probably serve God in our varied secular callings. Whether you own a business, work for others, or labor at raising your children, you have plenty of chances to live out your faith in God.

Regardless of what we do for God, the important thing to remember is that he designed us the way we are. We didn't make ourselves or create our own lives. Therefore, it's right for us to give our lives to God so that whatever we do, we live and act for his glory.

This passage from Jeremiah has been a powerful inspiration for members of the pro-life movement. The passage makes clear that human life is something that begins before birth, and possibly even before conception.

But the message of this passage is relevant to all of us, not just prophets and pro-life activists. God is trying to remind us that our lives are in his hands, and that he has cared for us since before there was an "us" to care for.

Our lives are part of a vast, seamless web of love and creation that began long before we were born. If we remember this, our lives can be transformed.

———

Thank you, God, for making me. Now help me serve you any way I can.

34

Chosen by Jesus

"Come, follow me," Jesus said, "and I will make you fishers of men."

Matthew 4:19

PETER and Andrew were two humble fishermen who left every-thing behind when Jesus called them to follow him. The Bible doesn't tell us the reaction of their families or friends at this strange behavior, but we can imagine that they found Peter and Andrew's sudden departure from their livelihood a bit surprising.

What must have been even more shocking was Jesus' ability to en-gender such wholehearted devotion. How amazing it must have been to be so drawn to Jesus that you dropped your life's work and went with him. And the term "fishers of men" must have seemed ter-ribly odd to those first disciples.

But they went. And as he began to teach, others followed him, too. The disciples were ordinary people who heard him and believed his message. Like fish gathered into a net, they came.

The disciples sat at his feet and learned how they, too, could tell others about him and communicate with power. They must have wondered sometimes why Jesus chose them. They were the most ordinary of men.

In many ways the disciples were just as we are today. We hear about Jesus, are drawn to him, accept him as our Savior, and then learn that we are to be fishers of men.

I remember the first time I was told that I could be a witness for Jesus. "Not me," I said.

It isn't that I was shy, but I was very afraid. I couldn't imagine someone like me, with no formal training in the Bible, no scholarly background or seminary training, telling others about Jesus with enough skill to change their minds.

But I did learn to fish for men. And I did grow in understanding that what I learned was useless unless the Holy Spirit came into each encounter and touched the heart of the listener.

It is thrilling to grasp that God has chosen ordinary men and women, just like the first disciples, to be instruments of his mercy; to be tools in the saving of souls from the time of the disciples and on into eternity.

The Savior of the world who walked beside the Sea of Galilee and called his early followers walks with us today and calls us into relationship with him. He gives us the power to touch the hearts of others and experience the joy of seeing them accept him.

How humbling.

———

Father, thank you that you draw us, call us, and use us in your service. We know you could have chosen other ways to bring the message of salvation to the world, but we are grateful that sometimes you bless us with that privilege.

35

Raising a Ruckus

David, wearing a linen ephod, danced before the LORD with all his might, while he and the entire house of Israel brought up the ark of the LORD with shouts and the sound of trumpets.

As the ark of the LORD was entering the City of David, Michal daughter of Saul watched from a window. And when she saw King David leaping and dancing before the LORD, she despised him in her heart.

2 Samuel 6:14–16

WHEN *Saturday Night Live* comedian Dana Carvey decided to create a character who parodied uptight religiosity, he called her the Church Lady.

The Church Lady was a grumpy, dowdy-looking woman who excelled at being holier-than-thou and confronted some of the guests on her fictional *Church Chat* show with comments such as: "Who do you think made you do that, maybe S-A-T-A-N?"

In an interview, Carvey said he based the character on a real woman he remembered from the Lutheran church in San Mateo, California, he attended as a child. "Even the most pious person, even the most straightforward Christian, has been a victim of hearsay and gossiping by condescending people," he said. "They're rampant everywhere, and not just in church."

Carvey's family attended church regularly, but not as often as some in the church thought they should. "I imagined people thinking, 'Well, apparently some of us care a little more about Christ than others!'"[1]

Even potluck dinners provided an opportunity for competition and judgmentalism. Carvey's memories inspired a *Saturday Night Live* episode in which the Church Lady, who had labored over an elaborate casserole, chided a fellow believer who brought lowly Jell-O.

Religious people sometimes confuse their own ideas with God's commands, and when they do, they place needless emphasis on external behavior and judging others.

David wasn't that kind of person, as anyone can tell you who has read his heartfelt prayers found in the Book of Psalms.

In the passage from 2 Samuel, David was so overcome with love for God that he praised him with an impromptu dance. Churches didn't exist in those days, but apparently his wife disliked David's exhibition and "despised" him for it.

David didn't let the episode bother him. In later passages, he remained a deeply emotional person, both in his relationships with other people and his worship of God.

Worship is a highly individualistic activity. But the single most important thing about worship isn't the particular form you follow, it is the attitude of your heart and soul.

David praised God as his heart deemed appropriate. If people around him judged him for his devotion, he wasn't worried. He knew God would honor his worship and understand the feelings that kindled his expression.

———

God, help me love you with all my heart and not worry about what people think.

36

The Wonderful Wisdom of God

Oh, the depth of the riches
of the wisdom and knowledge of God!
How unsearchable his judgments,
and his paths beyond tracing out!

Romans 11:33

WHEN I think back to my high school and college days in the 1960s, I marvel at how much things have changed.

I had an electric typewriter, which was a luxury, and a set of *World Book Encyclopedias*. We had no home computers, no laptops, no Internet. Writing research projects required many hours in the library and in correspondence with other institutions that might provide material pertinent to a subject.

Today, the availability of information is almost limitless. The Internet has revolutionized the time needed and the material accessible for the completion of projects or the satisfaction of curiosity.

I think the recent advent of technology has caused many of us to be uncomfortable with words and ideas like "unsearchable." How can anything be intellectually out of reach when the world of information lies beneath our fingertips?

Of course the intellect alone does not reveal the knowledge of God, and this is another uncomfortable thought for many twenty-first-century people. Even those of us who believe in him may find ourselves a little irritated with a verse like Romans 11:33.

Our irritation can turn into wonder if we recognize the amazing power that is available to us through faith and the working of the Holy Spirit. A God who is so wise and rich in knowledge loves us, died for us, has given us his Spirit. We can rest in his care and trust that what we don't know won't hurt us.

I have become comfortable knowing that God is even bigger than I can imagine, something I couldn't do if I didn't trust him.

It's like how I feel when I get on an airplane. I prefer not to see the pilot. I have enough trust to get on board, but I feel more confident if I imagine the pilot to be superhuman and flawless. I want him to be so perfectly competent that I'm comfortable with trusting him with my life.

This kind of thinking is just mental gymnastics to relieve fear, but the power of the Holy Spirit infuses my confidence that God is bigger than life. Planes do crash occasionally, but the "depth of the riches / of the wisdom and knowledge of God" remains an attribute that merits my trust in him.

I can grow to know him more and more as I mature in my faith, but I can also stand amazed that all the knowledge in this world doesn't come close to explaining how awesome he is.

––––––

Father, I thank you that you are bigger than we can ever imagine and that you still stoop down and love us unconditionally.

37

Cathedrals of the Heart

This is what the LORD says:
"Heaven is my throne,
and the earth is my footstool.
Where is the house you will build for me?
Where will my resting place be?
Has not my hand made all these things,
and so they came into being?" declares the LORD.
"This is the one I esteem:
he who is humble and contrite in spirit,
and trembles at my word."

Isaiah 66:1–2

ANYONE who has ever traveled Europe has seen beautiful, majestic cathedrals that Christians living in earlier centuries built to honor God. In such countries as Italy, France, and England, gigantic structures of stone, wood, and glass rise into the sky. Their construction required decades of work and dedication. When completed, their graceful spires towered over towns and could be seen miles away.

Today, skyscrapers and apartment complexes tower over many modern cities, but cathedrals still have a special power and grace.

Catholic scholar Robert Barron has written a beautiful little book called *Heaven in Stone and Glass*, which explores the marriage of theology and architecture that led to the creation of the York and Lincoln Cathedrals in England and three French cathedrals: Notre Dame, Chartres, and Le Mans.

"These cathedrals are powerful repositories of the Christian spirit," he wrote. "In their windows, towers, vaults, naves, roses, labyrinths, altars and facades, these Gothic churches bring the transformative energy of Jesus Christ to bear on our world."[1]

Visiting old cathedrals today can be a powerful religious experience. Many were built in the shape of a cross. And walking down their aisles toward their massive altars, one finds his eyes drawn heavenward by the towering stone columns and the stained glass windows that portray scenes from the Bible and the life of Christ.

But you don't have to travel to a European cathedral to worship God. Wherever you are right now as you are reading these words can be your own personal cathedral. A brief walk in a park or even a stroll down a sidewalk can expose you to some of the wonders of God's handiwork.

But the most important thing isn't your surroundings. It's the state of your heart. As Isaiah told us, the characteristics God esteems in those who would worship him are a humility and contriteness of spirit, and a respectful awe for his revealed Word.

Whether you're in a beautiful cathedral or your messy living room, God wants you to honor and acknowledge him as God.

———

God, I worship you. You are the Lord of the cosmos. Help me to understand and honor your majesty.

38

Taking Up Your Cross

Then he called the crowd to him along with his disciples and said: "If anyone would come after me, he must deny himself and take up his cross and follow me. For whoever wants to save his life will lose it, but whoever loses his life for me and for the gospel will save it."

Mark 8:34–35

HERE'S how German pastor Dietrich Bonhoeffer summarized the main point of the Christian life: "When Christ calls a man, he bids him to come and die."[1]

Bonhoeffer knew exactly what he was talking about. He lived in Germany during the troubled time when Hitler was growing more and more powerful and the dreaded Third Reich was re-creating German society in its evil image.

Many pastors supported Hitler, in part because it was easier being part of the officially approved church. But Bonhoeffer could see what many others didn't: that Hitler was evil, and that collaboration with the Third Reich would spell doom.

Bonhoeffer was one of the leaders in the Confessing Church Movement, an underground network of churches and seminaries that tried to stay true to the message of the gospel at a time of intense pressure to cave in and compromise.

As time passed and the world came ever closer to the brink of World War II, Bonhoeffer was invited to stay in America instead of returning to the chaos and turmoil of Hitler's Germany. But he decided to return and suffer alongside his fellow countrymen.

Finally, Bonhoeffer joined a plot to assassinate Hitler. The plot was uncovered, and Bonhoeffer was imprisoned in 1943. Nazis hanged him on April 9, 1945, three days before Allied troops liberated the prison camp where he was killed.

Even before he faced death, Bonhoeffer wrote about taking up the cross in his most famous book, *The Cost of Discipleship*: "Cheap grace is the deadly enemy of our church," he wrote. "We are fighting today for costly grace."

Bonhoeffer went on to give a more detailed description of what he meant by cheap grace: "Cheap grace means grace sold on the market like cheapjacks' wares. The sacraments, the forgiveness of sin, and the consolation of religion are thrown away at cut prices. Grace is presented as the Church's inexhaustible treasury, from which she showers blessings with generous hands, without asking questions or fixing limits. Grace without price; grace without cost!"

Today, one can find cheap grace in Christians who turn to Jesus seeking what he can do for them, not what they can do for him.

Cheap grace can also be found in sermons that emphasize "God has a wonderful plan for your life" but downplay the costs that come from true commitment.

Cheap grace can also be found when we ask Christ to grant us the power of his resurrection without enduring the pain of his crucifixion. As Bonhoeffer reminded us, "he bids [us] to come and die."

Jesus, you went to the cross for me. Help me take up my cross and serve you with my life.

39

Who Are You to Grumble to God?

Where were you when I laid the earth's foundation?
Tell me, if you understand.

Job 38:4

G RUMBLING to God is one of the world's most popular pastimes. People grumble to God when the temperature is too hot or too cold, and when it rains or snows too much or too little.

People grumble when the stock market goes down, or even when the "wrong" stocks go up at the "wrong" time.

And imagine how complex things get in the cases of competitions or wars in which one side wins and the other loses. Whether it's the Green Bay Packers *v.* the Pittsburgh Steelers, the Lakers *v.* the Nets, or the North *v.* the South in the Civil War, God often hears from roughly equal numbers of people on either side who are disappointed with how things turned out.

The Book of Job is full of grumbling. And who wouldn't complain if subjected to the kinds of trials and tribulations Job faced?

Job was a godly and prosperous man. But what happened when his prosperity disappeared and unimaginable suffering set in? Did he remain godly, or did he get angry and turn his back on God?

Readers can see for themselves. Job continued to honor God, often in spite of the misguided assistance his friends offered. They spent most of their time trying to persuade Job that his own sin brought on the many problems he was facing.

Finally, after thirty-seven chapters of humans' grumbling and blaming, God stepped in and let readers know what he thought about Job's predicament. God made his case by asking a series of probing questions:

- Where were you when I laid the earth's foundation?
- Who shut up the sea behind doors?
- Have you ever given orders to the morning or shown the dawn its place?
- Have the gates of death been shown to you?
- What is the way to the abode of light?
- Who cuts a channel for the torrents of rain and a path for the thunderstorm?
- Do you send the lightning bolts on their way? (Job 38: 4, 8, 12, 17, 19, 25, 35)

In other words, God had a simple message for Job or anyone who would question divine wisdom: "Look, you don't know what I know. In fact, you don't know even the half of it. So settle down. Quit your grumbling, and trust me."

Pain and suffering are powerful feelings. When our bodies are ailing, our minds are troubled, or loved ones are hurt or killed, it's difficult to continue trusting God.

God doesn't tell us to ignore our sufferings, or to pretend they don't exist. He just wants us to remember that he's God—we aren't—and grumbling isn't necessary.

And he wants us to remember that he's still in charge of the whole wide universe, including the little portion of it where we live.

———

Forgive me, Father, when I doubt your wisdom and sovereignty. Help me submit my stubborn will to your hands.

40

If God's in It, Stand Back!

Leave these men alone! Let them go! For if their purpose or activity is of human origin, it will fail.

Acts 5:38

THE person speaking these words in Acts 5 was Gamaliel, an honored Pharisee and one of the most famous teachers of the Law. Saul was one of his students (Acts 22:3).

The occasion was the apostles' (Peter and those with him, Acts 5:29) appearance before the Sanhedrin so the high priest could question them.

In the previous days, the apostles had been healing many people, and their fame was spreading throughout the land. The number of believers in Jesus multiplied as the apostles preached the gospel.

The Sadducees, priests who controlled the temple, were jealous of the apostles and had them arrested and put in jail.

Imagine the high priest's and his colleagues' surprise when they called for the apostles to be brought to them—but the apostles were nowhere in sight. The doors of the jail remained securely locked and guards were still on watch. But amazingly, the cells were empty.

While the Sanhedrin puzzled over this development, another person came running into the room and told them that the apostles were in the temple courts teaching the people. Guards brought the apostles back to appear before the high priest.

An angel of the Lord had miraculously released the apostles from the jail the night before. Of course, the Sanhedrin didn't know about the angel and remained perplexed as to how the apostles escaped, only to speak as publicly as they ever had about Jesus.

The Sanhedrin were furious when the apostles spoke boldly about their activities. Jesus' followers were open about their continuing plans to tell the people about the Savior and were unafraid of the consequences. They told the high priest that they must obey God rather than man (Acts 5:29).

The Sanhedrin wanted to put the apostles to death, but Gamaliel warned against such action.

Gamaliel reasoned, "For if their purpose or activity is of human origin, it will fail. But if it is from God, you will not be able to stop these men; you will only find yourselves fighting against God" (Acts 5:38–39).

This famous Pharisee acknowledged God's power, even though the apostles were teaching a doctrine that the leaders of the Jewish community had forbidden.

The Sanhedrin released the apostles after having them beaten and telling them, once more, not to speak in the name of Jesus. Of course the apostles ignored the command and joyfully continued to tell the people about Jesus. Gamaliel was right: God was with these men, and no one could stop them.

———

Father, help us to be bold in our own witness of your truth.

41

Music to Our Ears

A voice of one calling:
"In the desert prepare
the way for the LORD;
make straight in the wilderness
a highway for our God."

Isaiah 40:3

EVERY fall, choirs and orchestras around the world start rehearsing Handel's *Messiah,* one of the most celebrated musical compositions the world has ever heard. To show their respect for this exceptional work, audiences typically stand for the singing of the "Hallelujah Chorus," a tradition that began with British royalty.

For many people, the Christmas season would seem empty without a performance of the *Messiah.* But Handel, a devout Christian, always intended the work to be sung at Easter time.

If you haven't heard it, the *Messiah* is a beautiful retelling of the biblical story of Christ, beginning with the ancient prophecies about him and continuing through his death, resurrection, and ascension to heaven. Handel took the lyrics straight from the Bible, and many of them came from the Book of Isaiah, which contains some of the more interesting prophecies about Jesus. Even though Isaiah lived some seven centuries before the time of Christ, he accurately predicted much about Jesus' life and work.

The passage above is taken from Isaiah, and it describes the mission of John the Baptist. John had a unique assignment. He would baptize Jesus and then announce his arrival to the world.

We get a more complete description of John in the third chapter of the Gospel of Matthew, where he is described as a wild-eyed Jewish man who lived in the desert, surviving on a diet of honey and wild locusts. John and his small group of followers were trying to serve God as best they could, and when Jesus arrived on the scene, they could see that he was the promised fulfillment of centuries worth of pent-up longings and desires.

Over the centuries, Jewish prophets made numerous predictions about the coming Messiah. He would help people worship God with greater sincerity. He would forgive their sins. And he would help bridge the gap that had grown between God and the human race.

Jesus did all of these things, and Handel's *Messiah* tells the whole story in a beautiful oratorio that takes nearly three hours to perform.

The good news about Jesus has been changing lives for nearly two thousand years. And even the *Messiah* itself has had a powerful impact on many people.

According to Roger Bullard's *Messiah: The Gospel according to Handel's Oratorio*, Handel conducted the work at its debut performance in Dublin, Ireland, in April 1742. The concert was a benefit for people confined to a debtors' prison. The money that first performance raised enabled 142 men to leave the prison as free men.

Handel also set up a trust fund that benefits from the annual performances of the *Messiah*. The fund still supports a hospital for abandoned children in London.

The next time you hear a choir sing the "Hallelujah Chorus," I hope the beautiful music will help you think about the profound message of Christ's incarnation. Meanwhile, think about the many ways Christ's life and teaching have had a powerful, transforming impact on so many people for so long. This is truly music to our ears.

————

Father, thank you for coming to earth to reach people like me. And thanks for inspiring artists like Handel to retell your wonderful story.

42

A Miracle and a Meal

When Jesus came into Peter's house, he saw Peter's mother-in-law lying in bed with a fever. He touched her hand and the fever left her, and she got up and began to wait on him.

Matthew 8:14–15

SOME biblical miracles almost seem like they were created to light up the screens in movie theaters. Cecil B. DeMille's *The Ten Commandments* won an Academy Award for the special effects it employed to show the parting of the Red Sea and the writing of the Ten Commandments.

Other biblical epics portray some of the more dramatic moments from Jesus' life: the time he came to his disciples walking on the water; the day he fed five thousand people with a few fish and a few loaves of bread; and his forty days of temptation in the desert.

Here, Matthew gives us a passage that is so tiny and quiet that we almost overlook it. In these two verses, the miraculous and the mundane happen simultaneously. That's why you won't see this passage acted out in any major motion pictures. It's just too ordinary.

In the preceding chapters Jesus delivered his Sermon on the

Mount, one of the most important sermons ever delivered. Then in chapter eight and the following chapters, Jesus demonstrated what his new kingdom would look like by performing a variety of miracles.

Then, after healing a leper and the servant of a Roman official, Jesus did something we can all relate to. He went to Peter's house for a time of rest and relaxation. Perhaps Jesus needed to sit down and rest his tired and weary feet. Maybe it was a cup of water he needed most. Or perhaps he merely wanted a few moments away from the crowds that continued to throng around him and press in on him.

Peter had been one of the first men who agreed to follow Jesus, but he still had a family. This brief passage doesn't give us many details about the family life of the disciples, but I suspect that Peter's house was a lot like mine and yours: messy, active, and noisy.

But even in the midst of this private domestic scene, Jesus has an opportunity to demonstrate his divine power. Peter's mother-in-law is laid up with a fever, so Jesus touched her hand and healed her.

If this had been a movie, we would have expected a few angels to hover overhead flapping their wings while the soundtrack's violins played a crescendo of sound. Instead, the woman got up and began waiting on Jesus. Perhaps she even cooked him a batch of her favorite cookies.

These two verses are little more than a brief break in the action. Soon, the crowds will be gathering again, and Jesus will be performing more fantastic miracles such as healing the sick and casting out demons.

Movies will always focus on these dramatic scenes, but Jesus' visit to Peter's house reveals another side of the Savior. And through this humble domestic episode, shows us that God doesn't love us only in our most "religious" moments, but also when we're just hanging out in the family room with our family.

Jesus isn't some otherworldly deity who is insensitive to the daily reality of our lives. Instead, he comes into our daily lives and transforms the mundane existence into something miraculous.

————

Jesus, I thank you for coming to earth in human form, and I ask you to transform my daily life into an occasion for the miraculous.

43

Be Courageous

Be strong and courageous. Do not be terrified; do not be discouraged, for the LORD your God will be with you wherever you go.

Joshua 1:9

WE collided in the hallway, grabbing at each other with hearts racing. The blare of the burglar alarm had jolted my daughter Lisa and me out of our beds and toward each other as fear swept up the stairs like a chilling, permeating fog.

Frozen where we'd met, we waited, speechless, each of us trying desperately to quiet our panicked breathing. *Nothing*—we heard nothing but the incessant wail of the alarm.

After a seeming eternity, I motioned Lisa into my bedroom and over to the phone. We huddled together with eyes glued to the top of the stairs. I picked up the receiver, and the line was dead—no dial tone, just the vast silence of disconnection.

Had the intruder cut the line? Did a call get through to the monitoring service before the line was severed?

Lisa and I stared at each other, silently acknowledging our fear. Then we both softly whispered to God, "Father, help us."

The mere acknowledgment that God was near and could hear our prayer calmed our hearts. The alarm was still ringing and fear was still alive. But we now knew we were no longer alone in our fear.

Calmer, I picked up the receiver again. A dial tone buzzed. Our fears began to subside.

A call had gone through to the alarm monitoring company, and the police soon arrived. They found no sign of an intruder and assured us that it was just a glitch in the alarm system.

As frightening as that false alarm had been, Lisa and I could only imagine how much worse it would have been if either of us had been truly alone. How dark and engulfing our fear would have been without the knowledge that God was right there with us.

Joshua faced much more than a potential intruder to his camp. He was about to lead the children of Israel across the Jordan and into the promised land. He was following in the footsteps of Moses, a great leader now dead.

But God had spoken to him: "Be strong and courageous. Do not be terrified; do not be discouraged, for the LORD your God will be with you wherever you go."

God's promise to Joshua is God's promise to us. The power behind it gives us courage when we are afraid. It helps us keep going in the face of peril, whether actual or perceived threats to our physical, emotional, or spiritual well-being threaten to destroy our peace.

The power of God's presence turns even the darkest moments into opportunities to trust him with our very lives.

Whether we tremble in the dark or are moving into new and unknown territory, God goes with us, replacing our terror with trust.

———

Father, thank you for your continual presence in my life and the courage it gives me to face my deepest fears.

44

Adopted into God's Family

*Consequently, you are no longer foreigners and aliens, but fellow citizens
with God's people and members of God's household.*

Ephesians 2:19

THE Jews were God's chosen people. In Old Testament times only
the children of Israel enjoyed the benefits of covenant relationship with the one true God. Gentiles were outside of the promises of
God and without hope.

Then, through the redemptive blood of Jesus, the uncircumcised
became part of God's family.

This verse holds particular meaning for me, because I was adopted
into my own family. I don't know who my biological parents were, but
I know that my adoptive parents loved me with all their hearts. They
loved me not because I was born of them but because I became a part
of their family. I enjoyed all the rights and privileges that their own biological children would have. They never discriminated against me
because I was adopted.

The same is true for us. God loves us Gentiles as much as the children of Israel and he folded us into his family at the time of Christ.

It is difficult for us to fully appreciate what that adoption means, since most of us have little experience with being foreigners and aliens.

I have tried, in the past, to imagine what it would have been like to be in an orphanage with no family who wanted me. That was the fate of many children when I was growing up, but I can't even fathom how painful that kind of estrangement would have been.

The closest that I've come to feeling outside the norm has been when traveling in countries where English is not the national language. I remember my first trip to Germany. I was with several other people and we had rented a car to drive from Frankfurt to a small town near Düsseldorf.

Even with road maps we had a challenging time following directions. We often took the wrong exit off the major highways when driving through a town. Some people tried to be helpful but many just waved us away, unable to understand English. We certainly felt like the foreigners we were.

Much more consequential is the fact that we Gentiles were aliens to the family of God prior to the work of Jesus on the cross. It's one thing to be lost on a road in a foreign country and quite another to be a lost soul, without access to the Father.

How amazing that he chose to graft us into his family tree and bestow on us all the blessings of his children. The power of the cross was for the forgiveness of sins for the Jew and Greek, male and female, all who believe on his name.

Father, we are so grateful that you chose to include all who believe in Jesus as part of your family.

45

Aglow with God's Glory

When Moses came down from Mount Sinai with the two tablets of the Testimony in his hands, he was not aware that his face was radiant because he had spoken with the LORD.

Exodus 34:29

MOSES' face was so radiant that the Israelites were afraid to come near him (Exod. 34:30). He put a veil over his face and took it off again only when he was in the presence of the Lord.

Moses and God had met together many times before Moses' face took on such radiance. But this time something was different.

In chapter 19 for example, Moses went up Mount Sinai to meet with God, and "the LORD called to him from the mountain" (v. 3). Then God told Moses to go back and consecrate the people, for God would show himself to them in the form of a cloud over the mountain.

When God appeared, he displayed his power with a dense cloud, thunder and lightning, and the blast of a trumpet. The mountain shook, and the people trembled at the overwhelming force before them.

"Moses spoke and the voice of God answered him" (Exod. 19:19). Then he went up the mountain and spoke with God. When he came back down, he told the people not to approach Mount Sinai, for they could not see God and live.

In chapter 20 God once again appeared in the midst of a cloud, with thunder and lightning and the sound of a trumpet. Moses reentered the darkness of the cloud to meet with God.

In chapters 21–33 Moses had more divine encounters, getting closer to God than anyone else and receiving instructions to take back to the people. God himself inscribes the tablets of the Ten Commandments (Exod. 31:18).

Then in Exodus 33:18 the relationship changed. Moses boldly said to God, "Now show me your glory." The word *glory* here refers to something that is heavy, impressive, honored. Moses must have been asking to see God more fully than he already had.

And God agreed in part. God put Moses in the cleft of a rock, covered Moses with his hand, and passed by. As God moved away, he allowed Moses to see his back . . . in all God's glory.

Moses spent forty days and forty nights up on the mountain in the presence of God. It was at the conclusion of these forty days that Moses descended from the mountain and his face was radiant.

The Bible doesn't tell us exactly what changed between God and Moses that transformed the man's appearance. But it seems reasonable to assume that the radiance came from Moses' being in the presence of God's glory.

And in our own way, we can be transformed by the glory of God, too.

———

Father, we cannot imagine what it will be like to see you in all your glory, but we thank you that one day we will. We thank you that we will be fully in your presence.

46

From Religion to God

𑁍

Paul then stood up in the meeting of the Areopagus and said: "Men of Athens! I see that in every way you are very religious. For as I walked around and looked carefully at your objects of worship, I even found an altar with this inscription: TO AN UNKNOWN GOD. Now what you worship as something unknown I am going to proclaim to you."

Acts 17:22–23

SAINT Paul would have been fascinated by San Francisco, Boulder, Colorado, or Sedona, Arizona. Some celebrate these cities and others like them as New Age meccas where spiritually hungry people can constantly compare notes on the latest techniques designed for experiencing the transcendent or the true.

Paul traveled endlessly in his tireless effort to spread the message of Christ. And when he went to a new city, he didn't hide out in a Christian ghetto where things would be safe. He felt a burning passion to investigate people's diverse spiritual interests. In Athens, which was a thriving spiritual mecca of the ancient world, he spent part of a day examining the city's rituals and religious relics. "All the Athenians and the foreigners who lived there spent their time doing nothing but talking about and listening to the latest ideas" (Acts

17:21). Paul was particularly intrigued with an altar that was inscribed with these haunting words: "TO AN UNKNOWN GOD."

The next day, Paul spoke to the Areopagus, a group of spiritual seekers. He wanted to tell these people about Jesus, but he thought it would be better if he warmed up the crowd by first talking about some of their homegrown gods.

He talked about the inscription he had seen on the altar. He also quoted a line from one of the most famous Cretan poets: "For in him we live and move and have our being" (Acts 17:28). Then, unlike some preachers, Paul didn't say that the Athenians were nasty, evil people for having so many gods. Instead, he began by trying to build a bridge of mutual understanding: "I see that in every way you are very religious."

God made us with a God-shaped vacuum deep in our souls, but people fill that hole in a variety of ways. Paul paid due respect to the Athenians' deep religiosity, but then he turned the tables on them, declaring that their desperate search for God had gotten them only a few miles down a very long road. "Now what you worship as something unknown I am going to proclaim to you," he said, and he proceeded to tell them about Jesus.

Those of us today who are trying to talk to others about Jesus should follow Paul's example. Paul quoted poets of his day, but we could adapt his approach to the realities of our own world. Most of our city streets don't have altars to unknown gods, but our cities are home to a diverse mix of religious and spiritual groups. Perhaps we could learn more about what some of these groups believe in order to talk to their members about how their doctrines agree or conflict with the Christian message. As for poets, many cities offer regular poetry readings. But we might also want to consider studying pop music and movies for signs of spiritual life. These media didn't exist in Paul's time, but in our time they are some of the most important conveyors of spiritual messages. Paul spoke from the heart about his Savior, but he also used his head to try to connect with his listeners in a way that would make sense to them.

————

Father, help me build bridges to the people you want to reach instead of erecting barriers.

47

Words Hurt

The tongue also is a fire, a world of evil among the parts of the body. It corrupts the whole person, sets the whole course of his life on fire, and is itself set on fire by hell.

James 3:6

STICKS and stones may break my bones, but words will never hurt me." Many of us learned this little ditty as children and tried to believe it when someone said hurtful things to us. But as this verse in James proclaims, words are powerfully dangerous.

I grew up in a household with an angry father. He could be very loving and giving and then lash out with rhetoric that sent me cringing into my room. In his later years I learned of his abusive childhood that, no doubt, contributed greatly to his angry words all through his life.

Even knowing and understanding why my father was so mad so much of the time didn't lessen the sting of his words. I think I've cried more tears over the things he's said to me than over anything else.

As a result of bearing the brunt of repeated verbal anger, I am very sensitive to how people talk to one another. My daughters can tes-

tify to the strict upbringing they endured as far as how they talked
to anyone. They were not allowed to say "Shut up," "You're so stupid," or a menagerie of other phrases that were related to words that
had hurt me as a child.

I heard Maya Angelou, the poet and author, speak at a conference
a few years ago. She draws in her audience with her soft-spoken,
gracious words of wisdom. Her very manner was poetic and lyrical.

One of her examples about the use of words has stayed with me.
She told the audience that she doesn't allow people who are speaking unkindly about someone else to stay in her home. If she hears
someone speak that way, she asks him or her to leave!

She went on to explain that words, once spoken, can't be taken
back. They are out, living, and stick to the walls of the room like
germs. As I listened to her metaphor I felt as if so many of my father's
words had stuck to the walls of my soul. They have lost much of
their power, but the hurt from them has left scars.

God created us with the ability to speak. Scripture even refers to
Jesus as "the Word" (John 1:1) and says "the word of God" is
"sharper than any double-edged sword" (Heb. 4:12).

We have the power to be life-destroyers or life-givers with just the
words we speak. It is a tremendous responsibility to take these
words from James 3:6 and determine to tame our tongues.

———

*Father, thank you for the gift of language and the healing that our
words can give to others. Help us always to speak with concern for
the impact our words have on others.*

48

A Divine Blessing

The LORD bless you and keep you;
the LORD make his face shine upon you
and be gracious to you;
the LORD turn his face toward you
and give you peace.

Numbers 6:24–26

I⊤ had been a long and difficult journey. For forty years, the Israelites had wandered in the scorching deserts of the Middle East as they searched for the new homeland God had promised them.

Moses, their divinely ordained leader, claimed he was following God's orders. But over the past four decades there had been many times when he looked more lost than everyone else.

By the time the Israelites got to Mount Sinai, the holy mountain where Moses received the Ten Commandments from God, they numbered more than one million souls (Num. 1:46). To commemorate their efforts thus far, God gave them a special blessing.

God communicated these verses recorded in Numbers to Moses, who passed them on to his brother, Aaron, and Aaron's sons, who served as the Hebrews' first priests. Aaron and his brothers then communicated God's blessing to the people. After years spent in captivity in Egypt and years more spent wandering in the desert, the people received this divine blessing as a welcome relief.

The Bible is a book of many blessings. Some of them come directly from the mouth of God. Many others are human blessings. But the one thing they all have in common is that they are designed to confer a sense of grace and inspiration to the person receiving the blessing.

In Psalm 118:26, David said, "Blessed is he who comes / in the name of the LORD." The crowd repeated these words from the Old Testament when Jesus entered the city of Jerusalem on the first Palm Sunday (John 12:13).

In the Beatitudes, Jesus based one of the most important talks of his entire earthly ministry around a series of blessings: "Blessed are the poor in spirit"; "Blessed are those who mourn"; "Blessed are the peacemakers" (see Matt. 5).

Many of us have lost touch with the ancient practice of blessing others, even though we certainly need to be blessed as much as earlier people did. If someone sneezes, you might hear another person say, "Bless you," but many of us go through much of our lives without receiving blessings from or giving them to the people around us.

If you want to change that, try blessing loved ones or family members whenever you meet. This can take the form of an unspoken prayer for them, or it can be a brief but sincere comment: "God bless you."

Just about anyone or anything can be blessed, and the blessings can be offered in either informal or formal ways. Many people seek the prayers and blessings of friends before starting a new venture, such as a new job or a move to a distant city. In such cases, blessings can be a powerful source of comfort and reassurance. Some churches have more formal services for blessing a new house or new office space. In such cases, a priest visits the site and leads the occupants through a prescribed ritual. And once a year, many Anglican and Episcopal churches host blessing of the animals services to honor the legacy of St. Francis of Assisi, the Italian saint who had a deep love for creation.

In your own life, you may even want to try blessing the co-worker or boss who annoys you or the driver who cuts in front of you on the highway.

This may seem like a lot of work at first, but once you get in the swing of things, blessing others—and being blessed yourself—will become a bigger part of your life. And like the Israelites, you will find the kind words a healing salve during a tough journey.

———

Thank you, God, for blessing us, and help me to be a blessing to others.

49

A Prowling Predator

Be self-controlled and alert. Your enemy the devil prowls around like a roaring lion looking for someone to devour.

1 Peter 5:8

THE image in this verse of a roaring lion was particularly meaningful to friends of mine years ago in Ft. Lauderdale, Florida. One sunny, south Florida day, Tom and Nancy's (not their real names) little boy, David, was playing on the sidewalk in front of their home. They lived in a beautiful neighborhood with only one problem: the people across the street from them harbored a lion behind tall, stucco walls.

He was caged and supposedly unable to harm anyone. The legal system was moving slowly to force the removal of this wild creature from a residential neighborhood, but those efforts were too late for David.

Somehow the lion escaped from his cage, scaled the wall and ambled across the street toward David and his older brother, Bobby. The lion circled David and let out a roar. Bobby ran into the house, screaming for his parents.

Tom and Nancy ran outside and faced the horror of seeing David's head and shoulders trapped inside the lion's mouth. Without thinking about either danger or impossibilities, Tom gripped the lion's jaws and pried them open. David's limp body fell out of the lion's mouth and amazingly, the beast lost interest and walked back home.

David was rushed to the hospital and while being wheeled into the operating room, he asked his mom to sing "Jesus Loves Me" to him.

David survived, and everyone who heard about the event marveled at Tom's ability to open the jaws of a lion. Tom knew he didn't do that on his own and fully acknowledged the power of God to intervene in a miraculous way to save David's life. That day Tom accepted Christ into his heart with unspeakable thankfulness.

Few of us will have as graphic an example of the devil stalking about the streets of our hometowns, but we can all acknowledge the presence and power of evil in our world. Certainly we who are Americans tasted evil on that fateful day when we watched so many thousands of people lose their lives in the attacks on the World Trade Center.

But Satan doesn't always come with such definition. Subtle devices are his specialty. He uses discouragement, distraction, busyness, greed, selfishness, and a host of other means to wield his power.

The good news is that his power is limited. While Scripture reveals the power of the evil one, it also testifies that God's power is greater.

This verse tells us to be "self-controlled and alert." With protection against temptation and awareness of Satan's wiles, we do not need to fear the power of the roaring lion. Like Tom, we can experience supernatural strength in overcoming evil with good.

———

Father, we are so aware of evil when it comes in graphic ways, but we are sometimes unaware of the more subtle moves of the evil one. Help us to discern good from evil and protect us always.

50

Called and Equipped

The LORD said to [Moses], "Who gave man his mouth? Who makes him deaf or mute? Who gives him sight or makes him blind? Is it not I, the LORD? Now go; I will help you speak and will teach you what to say."

Exodus 4:11–12

IT was a tough assignment God gave Moses, a shy, quiet man who was having a tough time imagining himself as a public speaker, military commander, or charismatic political leader.

Pharoah had kept the nation of Israel—the people of God's own heart—prisoners in Egypt for years. They were enslaved and oppressed. But God had seen the sorrows of their lives and the back-breaking labor they endured. He had heard their cries and heartfelt prayers for help.

Now, finally, God planned to deliver them from Egypt and take them to "a land flowing with milk and honey" (Exod. 3:8). The only thing needed was a willing human collaborator. For some unknown reason, God chose Moses.

Moses listened as God explained his assignment. Moses would go to Pharaoh, the world's most powerful leader, and command him to set the Israelites free. Then Moses would lead the thousands upon thousands of people across the barren desert to the place God had chosen for them.

Moses was skeptical. "What if they do not believe me or listen to me and say, 'The LORD did not appear to you'?" (Exod. 4:1)

No problem, said God, who showed Moses all the miraculous power that would be at his disposal.

Still uncertain, Moses raised another objection: "O Lord, I have never been eloquent. . . . I am slow of speech and tongue" (Exod. 4:10).

Growing tired of Moses' objections and lack of faith, God responded, "Who gave man his mouth?" He then comforted Moses with the following assurance: "I will help you speak and will teach you what to say."

Have you ever sensed God calling you to do something that you felt was beyond your strength or abilities?

Maybe your divine assignment wasn't as daunting as Moses'. Perhaps it was something as simple as a tug at your heart telling you to help a street person instead of going out of your way to avoid him. Or perhaps your assignment came during a coffee break at the office when a co-worker talked about the grief a recent loss caused and you felt moved to offer words of comfort and spiritual insight.

Our divine assignments don't always have to be big and complicated. It's easy to place a phone call to a friend the evening before she has a doctor's appointment, but the comfort you can provide may help her sleep soundly that night. In other cases, we can best serve others by listening to what they have to say. The gift of listening is something we all possess, but most of us are too busy talking most of the time instead of really trying to hear what others have to say. Divine assignments can also arise from our life-experiences. Once you have gone through a particular trial and emerged safe and sound on the other side, you have a unique ability to provide inspiration and guidance to those who face similar challenges.

Too often, many of us are like Moses, who responded to his divine summons by saying, "O Lord, please send someone else to do it" (Exod. 4:13).

But there are some assignments that nobody but you can carry out. They won't always be easy, but as God reminded Moses, he will give us the help we need in order to carry out what he has called us to do.

———

Father, here I am. Use me to do your will, and give me the strength I need to do it.

51

Children of Faith

I have no greater joy than to hear that my children are walking in the truth.

3 John 4

My daughter Lara and I recently enjoyed a full day of shopping while I was visiting her in California. Her three toddlers, Lisa and twins Nathan and Cole, alternated taking turns in the double stroller and walking next to us.

We stopped in a jewelry store so Lara could show me a beautiful necklace in the shape of a cross that she was hoping would be a birthday present from her husband, Craig.

Lisa was sitting in the front of the stroller, peering into the jewelry case and listening to Lara's conversation with the saleslady. Lara gently draped the gold chain of the necklace over her fingers and let the cross dangle.

"That's a cross!" four-year-old Lisa exclaimed. "Mommy, that's a cross!"

"I know, honey," Lara said.

"That's what Jesus came to do, he came to do that, Mom," Lisa said, now standing on the footrest of the stroller as if in a pulpit all her own.

I smiled at Lara and felt tears rise up in my eyes as I witnessed the fruit of parents teaching their children the truth.

We now have seven grandchildren and relish so many wonderful times with them and their obvious Christian upbringing. It is difficult to think of anything more joyful than watching the truth spill out of them. They are fully normal kids with their fair share of mischieviousness, but they also soak up God's truth.

In this verse, John was writing to Gaius, a Christian in one of the churches of the province of Asia. John was apparently referring to converts or believers in his care. He had had word that Gaius was walking in truth and delighted in that good news.

God, in his providence, imparts truth in many ways: through his Word, through his presence in the Holy Spirit, through the words of pastors and teachers. And he uses all of us as his vehicles to impart truth to those close to us.

How wonderful it is that the Word of God has the power to change lives, even when delivered in the routine of parenting. I used very little formality when teaching my children biblical truth. I just tried to live in front of them what I talked to them about. As is usually the case in parenting, I didn't know just how much of what I said *stuck*.

It seems that a good deal of it did. Of course, they had many other godly influences in their lives, but I know that some of the truth they now live came from our time together as a family.

Whether we have children or not, we all have the means to impart truth. And then sometimes we are blessed to enjoy the fruit of our labor.

———

Father, it is such a joy to see others walk in truth. We thank you for using us to help impact others with your Word.

52

The Choice Is Yours

This day I call heaven and earth as witnesses against you that I have set before you life and death, blessings and curses. Now choose life, so that you and your children may live and that you may love the LORD your God, listen to his voice, and hold fast to him.

Deuteronomy 30:19–20

LIFE is full of choices, as anyone can see by taking a brief trip to a fast-food restaurant.

Would you like your burger well done or rare? Sesame seed or sourdough bun? Hot sauce or mild sauce? As for the fries, would you like regular fries or curly cheese fries?

Similar choices confront you at the grocery store. Simply trying to choose a breakfast cereal can turn into a complex decision-making process that requires a selection from among hundreds of varied choices.

Even watching television involves making choices. Decades ago, there were three major broadcast channels. Today, most cable services offer dozens of choices, and some satellite dish systems offer hundreds.

Sociologists have a term that describes our current abundance of options for everything from food to TV to spiritual paths and "lifestyle options." They say twenty-first-century people suffer from an afflic-tion called "overchoice."

Some choices aren't very important. There may be two or more dif-ferent routes you can take when you're traveling to the store or the kids' school, but you'll reach your destination sooner or later, whichever way you go.

In other cases, the decisions we make have important and possibly even life-changing consequences. Some TV shows are entertaining and possibly even thoughtful. Others are mind-numbing, soul-stunting ex-ercises in crassness and exploitation.

Perhaps the most important choices we will ever face are those re-curring issues where we must choose between life and death, blessings and curses.

Will the way you punish your child teach him to honor and obey authority, or will it cause resentment and rebellion?

Will the way you run your business be a testimony to your depen-dence on God, or will it be a declaration of your complete dedication to looking out for yourself?

Will your decisions about everything from the fate of unborn chil-dren to the health of the environment reflect your concern with life, or will you unconsciously be using your God-given free will to support a culture of death?

The options are clear and the consequences—unlike those at fast-food restaurants—are significant. Now it's up to us.

———

God, thank you for the gift of free will. Help me use it wisely by making the right choices.

53

We Know the Final Victor

The revelation of Jesus Christ, which God gave him to show his servants what must soon take place. He made it known by sending his angel to his servant John.

Revelation 1:1

I REALLY don't want to know what will happen in the future. We know that we will have to pass through the valley of the shadow of death, but to know just when might rob us of beautiful days living in the present. I recently spoke with a widow of 9/11 who shared about the wonderful evening she and her husband had on September tenth.

"How different it would have been," she said, "if we knew we only had that night left together. It would have taken our joy away."

Of course, many people suffer from illness that leads to the inevitable day of parting, but we still do not know the exact time.

Having said all this, I also have to admit that I find great comfort in the Book of Revelation. Oh, a lot of it describes terrible things that will happen, but in the end, God is the victor.

I remember hearing Dr. Howard Hendricks speak years ago about sometimes being away from his home in Dallas on days when the

Dallas Cowboys football team was playing. He talked about his excitement over their games and what a fan he was.

He would have someone tape the game for him when he was away, and then he could watch it when he got home. Most of the time, he would hear the final score before he got home. Still, while watching the game he'd get engrossed in the plays as if they were happening in the present moment.

If the Cowboys were behind, Dr. Hendricks talked of being worried . . . until he remembered the final score (for games they had won, of course). Even when it looked really bad, he could hold on to the fact that they had already won.

He went on to tell us that he felt that way about heaven. We as believers know the final score. We win.

The Book of Revelation opens up some of the future to us and tells us not only the battles that lie ahead, but the final result. The apocalyptic language of Revelation helps us see events with a new set of eyes. It promises that God's power will ultimately defeat the forces of evil.

What a gift to know that we have the victory won, especially when times are difficult.

John received a glimpse that he shared with us, and we can hold on to it as all the information we need until time as we know it ends.

Father, thank you for revealing to us the final battle results. Thank you for being with us in our suffering and for giving us a picture of life's events from a heavenly perspective. Help us keep that perspective in view.

54

Being Like Children

But Jesus called the children to him and said, "Let the children come to me, and do not hinder them, for the kingdom of God belongs to such as these."

Luke 18:16

THIS past summer we enjoyed a reunion back on the East Coast with members of our extended family. Steve and I shared a beach house with our two daughters, their husbands, and seven children from both families plus a few others.

We all talked about how to have a good time and not get on each other's nerves, and how to give the six boys and one girl room to be kids and enjoy themselves.

Steve and I had a laid-back role as the older couple, not directly responsible for anyone and able to enjoy everyone. We knew it would be chaotic and noisy and that toys would be everywhere. *Let's just relax and let the good times happen*, we told ourselves. And so we did.

It was an absolutely wonderful week. The children all got along with each other and the adults were less uptight than they were at home.

We went to the beach most days and built sand castles and collected shells. At least one person always had a little one to keep track of since we were near the water's edge. The children were safe and at the same time had the space and time and energy to really relish life.

Sometimes one of them would become engrossed in digging for creatures, and he'd want the solitude to do it alone. At other times several of them would play with buckets and shovels and create their own imaginary constructions.

Why does the kingdom of heaven belong to those who are like little children? I think it must mean that we will all be most completely who God intended us to be without the inhibitions of adulthood. We will be less guarded, knowing that we are safe in God's care. We won't have to be like everyone else but will be free to express ourselves in unique ways.

Since the Bible tells us there will be no more tears in heaven (Rev. 21:4), it must mean that we will laugh in the reckless way that children laugh. They giggle with delight and double over with peals of joy.

There must be a lot of power that infuses our souls when we get to heaven to open up some of us to godly abandonment. Just to be free and childlike sounds like a tall order for many of us.

And I think God wants us to experience more of this godly abandon here on earth. On a vacation we can experience life without the responsibilities and restraints of daily life.

But what if we could be who God intended us to be all the time, not just on vacation? Maybe if we infused our souls with the nurture of God's love more frequently, we'd experience more fulfillment, laughter, and childlike peace.

God's nurture comes from worship, time with him, time with other believers, prayer and just thinking about how much God loves us, how much he wants to hold us the way we hold the little people in our lives.

And when the sun goes down and little people wind down they cuddle safely in the arms of those who love them. I can't think of much that is more peaceful than rocking a baby or an active toddler who gives in to sleepiness.

————

Father, thank you for the hope children give us that we will all laugh again in the innocence of younger days. Help us to be more relaxed in your love.

55

Hey, You: Listen to What I'm Saying!

Fix these words of mine in your hearts and minds; tie them as symbols on your hands and bind them on your foreheads. Teach them to your children, talking about them when you sit at home and when you walk along the road, when you lie down and when you get up. Write them on the doorframes of your houses and on your gates, so that your days and the days of your children may be many in the land that the LORD swore to give your forefathers, as many as the days that the heavens are above the earth.

Deuteronomy 11:18–21

If you've ever been to New York or Jerusalem, you may have seen devout Orthodox Jews whom you recognized by their long beards, flowing hair, black hats, and dark clothing.

In some cases, you even saw phylacteries—small leather boxes containing pieces of paper with biblical passages written on them. Orthodox men wear phylacteries strapped to their heads and arms during their weekday morning prayers to remind them of their duties to God and God's Word.

Passages such as this one from Deuteronomy inspire such devotion. This is from Moses' farewell address to the people of Israel. Moses had led these people for decades during their wanderings through the desert. Now he was dying, and it was time to pass on some final words of wisdom.

Two of the major themes Moses talked about were God's love for humanity and humanity's need to obey God. Moses also challenged people to study and follow God's Word.

Often when he spoke, Moses was speaking God's words. In this passage, there was one simple message God wanted to communicate: "Hey, you: listen to what I'm saying, and take it seriously."

Orthodox Jews who wear phylacteries are taking God seriously. So are committed Christians who try to organize their daily lives around the principles the Bible spells out.

The man who does the right thing at work when others encourage him to take an ethical shortcut is fixing God's Word in his heart.

So is the woman who perseveres in doing good even when she gets no credit for it.

So is the child who obeys her parents even if the commands they give aren't always fun to carry out.

Life can be so crazy and hectic that people often forget to do what's right and best. That's why God continually reminds us to focus our attention on the one true rule of life and conduct that he, the Creator of the cosmos, authored.

When we hear and obey what God says, our lives will be blessed. When we forget things that are truly important to focus on things that are merely urgent, we go off course.

————

Okay, God. I'm listening. Tell me what you want me to do and help me do it.

56

Seekers Will Find

Blessed are those who hunger and thirst for righteousness,
for they will be filled.

Matthew 5:6

THINKERS who study contemporary spiritual life have declared ours to be a "seeker culture."

Sociologist Wade Clark Roof interviewed hundreds of people for his book, *A Generation of Seekers: The Spiritual Journeys of the Baby Boom Generation*. Roof said many of the 76 million people born between 1946 and 1964 are asking deep questions about the meaning of life and are seeking spiritual answers to these questions. But unlike their parents, many are looking outside the walls of churches for their salvation.

Some look to close-knit circles of friends that provide the kinds of community and support that many Christians seek in churches. Others head to the great outdoors, where they experience a sense of closeness to God that they can't find in even the most majestic cathedrals. Others see signs of the divine in books, movies, and art. And still others seek answers in New Age books and an experience of the supernatural in assorted spiritual rituals and nostrums. Such searching isn't always successful, but many seekers remain confident that such quests for the sacred are more likely to bring them the experiences they long for than they would ever find in a church.

"Boomers still feel some 'distance' from almost every institution, whether military, banks, public schools, Congress, or organized religion," he wrote. "For many, having any kind of relationship with a religious institution is problematic."[1]

Jesus would have understood today's spiritual seekers. When he looked at the religious institutions of his own day, he saw a greater emphasis on outward forms of religiosity than on the inner dimensions of spirituality that give life meaning.

Christ saw hypocrisy nearly everywhere he looked. In fact, the word *hypocrites* turns up more than a dozen times in his teachings found in the Gospel of Matthew.

In Matthew 6, Jesus instructed his followers not to worship like the hypocrites, who stood on the street corners and prayed loudly to impress others with their religiosity. Instead, when you pray, he said, go into a room by yourself, close the door, and pray quietly to God, who will hear and answer your prayers (v. 6).

In Matthew 23, Jesus launched into a scathing critique of religious hypocrites. "Everything they do is done for men to see," he said. Then he unleashed a series of condemnations that began with the words "Woe to you." Along the way he referred to scribes and Pharisees—the religious leaders of his day—as "blind guides" (v. 16) and "a brood of vipers" (v. 33), among other colorful terms.

But Jesus wasn't all doom and gloom. Even though many people used religion as a way to avoid coming into contact with the living God, others had better results. "Blessed are those who hunger and thirst for righteousness," he said, "for they will be filled."

All of us have experienced hunger and thirst. For most of us, they are a mild discomfort we feel between meals, snacks, and coffee breaks. But those who have gone longer than normal without food and water really know what hunger and thirst can mean.

Jesus wants us to seek God with the same single-minded determination we would use to seek for food if we had gone without it for a week. We are all to be part of a "seeker culture." If we do that, he promises that we will find the spiritual nourishment we crave.

————

Father, thank you for making me hungry for you, and help me to continue seeking after your truth.

57

Sheep Have the Right-of-Way

The LORD is my shepherd,
I shall not be in want.

Psalm 23:1

STEVE and I headed out of the parking lot at the Dublin airport in our rental car. We knew that driving on the left side of the road would take some adjustment, but the narrowness of the roads was a surprise.

About twenty miles from the airport our dual highway faded away, and we found ourselves on our first highly anticipated Irish country road. I screamed at Steve to move more to the center as bramble bushes almost whisked against my window. Of course, he couldn't move more to the center or he would have hit oncoming cars.

As we rounded a corner, a scene this city girl would never have imagined halted our progress completely. A flock of sheep meandered along the road, jostling for position as they squeezed out of a gate on our right and turned onto the road ahead of us.

A man at the front of the flock was yelling back to them and his black-and-white dog scurried around the edges of the flock, nudging the sheep to move along.

We inched along behind them for about ten minutes. It was a fascinating sight, and we laughed at the reality of these dirty, smelly animals presiding over a public thoroughfare. Just as we began to wonder where they were going and how long it would take them to get there, their shepherd opened a gate on the left side of the road. The sheep crowded to rush through to the grassy meadow.

By the time they had all moved from one field to another, lines of backed-up traffic flowed in both directions. The shepherd waved to us and smiled and closed the gate behind the last of his flock.

This twenty-first-century encounter with a shepherd brought a smile to my spirit as I thought of the familiar words to the opening verse of the Twenty-third Psalm: "The LORD is my shepherd, I shall not be in want."

But as I watched the Irish shepherd I realized that I don't often bring the reality of the Lord as my own Shepherd into my daily life. In the most humble ways this Irishman cared for his sheep. And he did it in a way that presumed that everyone understood that the sheep had precedence over the cars on the road.

We are the sheep of our Father. He cares for us in the most basic, as well as the most profound, ways.

———

Father, thank you for your personal care, as tender as that of a shepherd tending his sheep.

58

The Warrior's Psalm

The LORD is my rock, my fortress and my deliverer;
my God is my rock, in whom I take refuge.
He is my shield and the horn of my salvation, my stronghold.
I call to the LORD, who is worthy of praise,
and I am saved from my enemies.

Psalm 18:2–3

BOB Boardman was a member of the U.S. First Marine Division fighting in the Pacific during World War II. Serving as part of a tank crew on the Pacific island of Peleliu, he found dread a constant companion.

"It was a fearful place," he says. "The island was a big coral rock, and the Japanese were hidden away in five hundred coral caves, both natural and man-made. We had to rout out the enemy cave by cave."

When he had a spare moment, Boardman consoled himself by reading the small Bible he had been given. As he made his way through the Psalms, he found solace in one particular passage that spoke to his fears.

It was Psalm 18, and an introductory note indicated the conditions under which it was written: "David sang to the LORD the words

of this song when the LORD delivered him from the hand of all his
enemies and from the hand of Saul."

Boardman called David's words his constant refuge on Peleliu.
Daily he faced the challenge of placing his ultimate faith in God, his
Rock, rather than being intimidated by the rock caves in which dan-
ger dwelt.

He still refers to the passage as "the warrior's psalm" and turns to
it often, both when he is speaking to the public and when he seeks
reassurance of God's presence in his life.

The opening lines of the psalm reveal that David was familiar with
the fears that beset soldiers. But mixed with his fears were notes of
hope and confidence in God, his Redeemer:

> The cords of death entangled me;
> the torrents of destruction overwhelmed me.
> The cords of the grave coiled around me;
> the snares of death confronted me.
> In my distress I called to the LORD;
> I cried to my God for help.
> From his temple he heard my voice;
> my cry came before him, into his ears. (Psalm 18:4–6)

Centuries before modern warfare turned Asia and Europe into
killing grounds, David's psalm conveyed the horrors of war: "The
earth trembled and quaked, / and the foundations of the mountains
shook" (v. 7). It's been said that war is hell, but Boardman's experience during World War II demonstrated to him that even in the
chaos and carnage of warfare, those who trust God can experience a
foretaste of heaven: "He reached down from on high and took hold
of me; / he drew me out of deep waters. / He rescued me from my
powerful enemy" (vv. 16–17).

For Bob Boardman and many others who've seen the cruel face of war, the assurance of God's presence has been a powerful spiritual lifeline.

———

Father, in the midst of life's turmoil and strife, help me place my trust in you.

59

Developing a Long View

He who was seated on the throne said, "I am making everything new!"
Then he said, "Write this down, for these words are trustworthy and true."

Revelation 21:5

THE beauty of our world is tainted by the ugliness we see all around us. Headlines shout the carnage that man thrusts upon man.

Several years ago Steve and I visited Israel. We traveled to Tiberius, on the Sea of Galilee, and spent several days touring that area. It was beautiful and peaceful—except for the reminder of trouble when we saw machine-gun toting soldiers standing on street corners.

We also visited Jerusalem, staying in a lovely hotel that was within walking distance of many sites. The city bustled with activity as Jewish and Arab people comingled.

One night we walked the streets of a local shopping area and watched Jewish teenagers hanging out in a pizza shop and coffee-houses, much the same way kids all over the word congregate with friends.

A few months later, we learned that a suicide bomber blew apart the pizza shop in that area. We had been right there. Those laughing youths we saw might have been in the midst of the terror.

Then on September 11, 2001, terror hit America, sending waves of concern across a land that such attacks had not touched.

Battles rage. Cities are destroyed. People kill each other and do much of the terror in the name of God, or a god.

Where is our hope?

This verse from Revelation tells us. It declares that God himself will make everything new. "He will wipe every tear from their eyes. There will be no more death or mourning or crying or pain for the old order of things has passed away" (Rev. 21:4).

We are now living under the old order. Satan infiltrates our world. Sin works its destruction. God is available to any who earnestly seek him, but many do not.

But we have a wonderful promise when the end of this world as we know it comes about. God will make everything fresh, untouched by sin, perfect.

I think that God gave this message to John and commanded him to write it down so that we would not lose hope. When we become discouraged or afraid, we can fix our eyes ahead—develop a long view—and see that evil will not win out in the end.

God will one day unleash his power on all of the world and he will emerge the victor. In that we can have great hope.

Knowing that evil's power is limited, we can look past the present with all its harrowing images of oppression, war and evil men. We can place our hope in the promises of God, grieve for the troubles of the moment but raise our eyes and our hearts to the reality of an awesome God who will work all things to his good.

———

Father, our world seems so much more dangerous than it did a few years ago. Our eyes have witnessed the horror that man can do to man. Please help us to keep hope alive by looking beyond the devastation to you. Thank you for your promises and the future we have waiting for us.

60

Making the Most of Your Opportunities

Seek the LORD while he may be found;
call on him while he is near.

Isaiah 55:6

HAVE you ever been to a store or post office where customers take a number and wait in a long line until the number is called?

One cold and snowy December day, I journeyed to a local post office carrying a mound of boxes full of Christmas presents for far-away family and friends. Entering the crowded waiting room, I struggled with my boxes and extended a hand to grab a number from the dispenser near the front door. I pulled number 94. The sign above the counter, where four busy employees were moving as fast as they could, said the latest number called was 52.

Usually when I go to the post office, I take something to read with me just in case. This time I had forgotten, which was too bad, because I probably could have read significant portions of Tolstoy's mammoth *War and Peace*.

The milling crowd of customers moved with geologic slowness. After I had been waiting for half an hour, the sign above the counter said "Now Serving: 74." By the time the workers were up to the mid-eighties, I felt like I was in a slow-motion daze. Then the next thing I knew, I looked up and the sign said 96.

After waiting for more than an hour, I had missed my turn.

During my long wait, I wondered if the scene I saw at the post office was anything like what God must deal with on a daily basis as he tries to answer the prayers of millions of people around the world.

But God isn't like a harried postal worker. God is omnipresent (he is everywhere at once). God is omniscient (he knows everything—including all the prayer requests people make *even before* they pray). God is omnipotent (he is all-powerful).

Still, Isaiah suggests there are times when we can't find God, as if like a busy postal worker he had hung up his "Out to lunch" sign.

But God isn't ever unavailable. Isaiah's book repeatedly shows that God makes himself available to us, even when we don't take advantage of the opportunity.

God isn't out to lunch, but there are plenty of times when we are. Perhaps we become too overwhelmed with the cares of daily life. Or perhaps we become so busy that we don't take thirty seconds to listen to God's still, small voice speaking in our hearts.

God is always here, even if our own attitudes and behavior make him seem a million miles away. He is always calling our "number."

———

Father, thank you for being there for me. Help me not to take you for granted.

61

Sins As Scarlet

The teachers of the law and the Pharisees brought in a woman caught in adultery. They made her stand before the group and said to Jesus, "Teacher, this woman was caught in the act of adultery. In the Law Moses commanded us to stone such women. Now what do you say?" They were using this question as a trap, in order to have a basis for accusing him.

But Jesus bent down and started to write on the ground with his finger. When they kept on questioning him, he . . . said to them, "If any one of you is without sin, let him be the first to throw a stone at her." . . . Jesus straightened up and asked her, "Woman, where are they? Has no one condemned you?"

"No one, sir," she said.

"Then neither do I condemn you," Jesus declared. "Go now and leave your life of sin."

John 8:1–11

It's a scandalous story set in seventeenth-century Boston. A married woman named Hester Prynne has an adulterous affair with a young pastor named Arthur Dimmesdale.

Author Nathaniel Hawthorne's *The Scarlet Letter* shows us how the religious leaders of Boston dealt with adulterers. In the case of Hester Pyrnne, they made her wear a red letter A on her clothing. No

When Being Good Isn't
Good Enough

The heart is deceitful above all things
and beyond cure.
Who can understand it?

Jeremiah 17:9

J EREMIAH, the so-called weeping prophet, here delivered one of the downbeat lessons for which he was so famous.

While some prophets repeatedly told people about the many good tidings God had in store for them, Jeremiah's messages to the residents of Jerusalem were more depressing. His usual point was this: "People, you have really messed things up this time, and you better get right with God. Now!"

One of the themes of Jeremiah's book is sin, a subject that wasn't any more popular in his day than it is in ours. Jeremiah preached to people who believed themselves to be God's chosen people. Their spiritual pride blinded them to their sin.

Centuries later, people remain blind to sin. Today a "therapeutic"

one discovers Dimmesdale's complicity until later in the story, so
didn't have to wear a symbol that others could see. Still, his guilt a
shame haunted him in other ways.

In this fascinating scene from John's Gospel, a small letter A is
enough to publicly condemn a sinner for her sexual misdeeds.

You've got to hand it to the Pharisees. They were tough on si
at least some sins, and at least those sins that were committee
others. In this case, the target was an easy one: a woman who
been caught in adultery.

The stage was set for another in the ongoing series of encou
between Jesus and the religious leaders of his day. As usual,
rose to the challenge, telling the Pharisees they could go ahea
stone the woman. But Jesus wanted the first stone to be throw
man who had never sinned. All the righteous indignation an
emotion that had been growing to a fevered pitch was now
tured by one simple statement.

Once the Pharisees had been dealt with, Jesus turned
woman, who probably still wore the look of one facing exe
Jesus was well aware of her sins, but he looked beyond these
tions to her heart, which was hungry for salvation. He forg
woman, commanding her to sin no more.

In our day, sexual sins continue to arouse the anger of n
cerned about righteousness and obedience to God's law. That
and good, but in pursuing righteousness, we also need to re
grace and forgiveness, or else we will wind up as self-deceiv
Pharisees.

———

*Father, I thank you for the gift of your forgiveness. Help m
ceive it for my own sins and to extend it to others when th
it, too.*

gospel says people are really good at heart if you can bring their many psychoses and addictions under control. That, combined with a billion advertising messages that preach some variation of the message "You deserve a break today," have led many to believe that they're really not so bad after all.

Some people even reject the very idea that there is any such thing as absolute good or evil. The concept of sin is seen as even more problematic. Others accept notions of good and evil but try to explain away their guilt and shame by pinning it on others. Instead of accepting blame for their misdeeds, they attribute their acts to abusive parents ("I wouldn't be so selfish if my daddy had loved me"), insensitive spiritual leaders ("I'm just trying to recover the sense of self-esteem that was beaten out of me by Sister Margaret in the fifth grade") or complaints about economic injustice that would make Robin Hood blush ("Yes, I downloaded dozens of copyrighted songs from the Internet without paying for them, but the music industry is a hugh international conglomerate that charges too much for CDs and will never miss a few dollars here and there").

Jeremiah would disagree. Called by God to convey God's message to a wayward world, Jeremiah preached a hard-edged message of repentance. People are sin sick, he said, and the only thing that can help them is God's loving grace.

Although he lived long ago, Jeremiah had a very contemporary approach to getting his message across. British author Steve Turner, who writes about art, says Jeremiah was one of the first conceptual artists because he regularly staged dramatic presentations to drive home his points. "Jeremiah hid his underwear in a crevice until it rotted and then displayed it as an illustration of how God saw Israel's pride," wrote Turner in his 2001 book, *Imagine: A Vision for Christians in the Arts*.

Centuries after Jeremiah, Jesus preached a message of love and grace, but his sermons didn't neglect the important subjects of human sin and pride. More recently, writer Frederick Buechner described sin as a destructive centrifugal force:

> When at work in a human life, it tends to push everything out toward the periphery. Bits and pieces go flying off until only the core is left. Eventually bits and pieces of the core go flying off until nothing is left. "The wages of sin is death" is St. Paul's way of saying the same thing.[1]

Buechner concluded his mini-essay on sin by saying: "More even than hunger, poverty, or disease, [sin] is what Jesus said he came to save the world from."[2]

"The heart is deceitful," said Jeremiah. And the more we try to argue with him, the more we reveal the truth of what he said.

———

Father, help me to see my sinful condition as clearly as you do. And please cleanse and purify my twisted little heart.

63

Use Me

"I am the Lord's servant," Mary answered. *"May it be to me as you have said."*

Luke 1:38

I WISH I could have been there to see Mary's face the day the angel came to her and announced that she would be giving birth to the Son of God. Did she wonder if she was losing her mind? Did she think some mischievous neighborhood children were playing a trick on her?

Luke tells us that she "was greatly troubled." Even the angel could tell she was upset. "Do not be afraid, Mary," he told her, "you have found favor with God" (Luke 1:29–30).

Like many faithful Jews, Mary had been eagerly waiting for the long-promised Messiah. But the angel's announcement that her womb would be the channel the Son of God would use to come into the world must have been shocking.

The first question Mary had concerned logistics. "How will this be, since I am a virgin?" The angel explained that "the Holy Spirit will come upon you, and the power of the Most High will overshadow you" (Luke 1:34–35). Though confusing, this answer was good enough for Mary. "I am the Lord's servant," she answered. "May it be to me as you have said."

I bet angels wish more human beings were as cooperative as Mary. The Bible is full of stories of people who resisted the call of God on their lives. Mary's willingness to submit to God's will shows why Christians throughout the ages have had a special respect for her.

The most famous disobedient Bible character is Jonah, who turned his back on God's call and suffered the consequences (see reading number eighty-eight, pages 202–203). But Jonah isn't alone. Old Testament figures like Moses, David, and Solomon resisted God's demands and saw their leadership ability severely hampered. In the Gospels, the disciples repeatedly failed to live up to Jesus' expectations. And in Acts chapter five a couple named Ananias and Sapphira tried to cheat the church. The couple had pledged to share all their worldly wealth with the Christian church that arose in Jerusalem after the resurrection of Christ. But after they received a windfall from a real estate deal they tried to hide their earnings from their fellow believers. Both Ananias and Sapphira "fell down and died" after their disobedience was revealed.

Mary's case is an unusual one. It's not every day that God wants a human being to give birth to his Son. But her attitude is an example for us all.

What might God want to do through you? And what will your response be when his angels come knocking at your door?

Maybe there's a sad and lonely person in your town whom God would like to reach, but he wants to reach him through you. Maybe there's a widow weeping over her loss, and God wants to comfort her through you.

Maybe there's a local soup kitchen that needs another pair of hands to prepare warm meals for cold and hungry people. Maybe

there's a Sunday school class that needs a teacher, or a nursery that needs another person to attend to toddlers.

You may never know all the fulfillment God has in store for you unless you open your heart as Mary did and submit to his higher purposes for your life.

God will not call on you to give birth to the Messiah, but you might just be the warm heart and tangible physical presence God needs to express his love to someone who could use it right now. Your deeds may not be recorded in the Bible or read by millions of people for thousands of years. But God will know what you've done, and that will be more than enough.

———

God, use me for your purposes. Show me what you want me to do.

64

Remembering What God Has Done

And tell them to take up twelve stones from the middle of the Jordan from right where the priests stood and to carry them over with you and put them down at the place where you stay tonight.

Joshua 4:3

T HE children of Israel once again crossed through waters God parted as the Jordan River opened before them. As soon as all had safely passed, the waters of the Jordan returned to flood stage.

Joshua had commanded one man from each of the twelve tribes to take a stone from the riverbed and bring it with him as he came out of the water. They carried the stones to Gilgal on the eastern border of Jericho, where Joshua erected the stones in a memorial.

He told the Israelites to teach their descendants that this pile of ordinary river stones symbolized God's faithfulness as the people had crossed the Jordan, just as he had demonstrated his faithfulness when they had crossed the Red Sea.

Why is it important to preserve a record of God's dealings with us? I think we need reminders of the unchanging faithfulness of God as we live in a world that is ever changing. As we read the Bible it reminds us of just how omnipotent God is. His hand stretches back through all of history and forward into all of the future.

But sometimes we forget. Or our stories of God's faithfulness lose their focus as one generation retells them to the next. When we go through long periods of time when God seems distant, doubts can disrupt our faith, and we may wonder how we felt when God's power was evident.

Just as the twelve stones from the river Jordan aided the Israelites' memories, the memorials we make enliven our memories.

One of the ways that I am trying to preserve family memories that are laced with touches from God's hand is to make creative photo albums. I am not a "crafty" person, but I have found great fulfillment in turning a collection of photos into a storybook that not only displays pictures but records what is happening during family times together.

I am hopeful that generations from now my descendants will look through these books and see the evidence of a family who loved God and lived in ways that acknowledged his presence in their lives. Memorials can be journals or collections of writings or art work— any number of things that express the reality of the presence of God in the life of an individual or family.

Whatever they are, they can be like the twelve smooth stones from the Jordan that bring us back to a time of experiencing the power of God in our lives.

———

Father, thank you for the ways that memories of your working in our lives can encourage us in the present moment. Help us to preserve them for future generations.

65

The Greatest Thing

And now these three remain: faith, hope and love. But the greatest of these is love.

1 Corinthians 13:13

M USICIANS such as country star Alan Jackson and rocker Bruce Springsteen wrote songs about the grief and sorrow the terrorist attacks on New York's World Trade Center caused. Jackson's *Drive* album featured the song "Where Were You (When the World Stopped Turning)?" Springsteen's album, *The Rising*, a recording permeated with Christian themes, included a song called "Into the Fire," which praised the bravery and sacrifice of those people who went into the World Trade Center buildings to save others.

Both songs quote 1 Corinthians 13, which is probably one of the most moving and famous passages of the entire Bible.

Paul wrote 1 Corinthians around A.D. 56. It was one of his many letters to the new Christian congregations that had sprung up in the decades since the death and resurrection of Jesus.

If there is such a thing as a perfect church, it doesn't appear in the pages of the New Testament. Sure, the Book of Acts records the dedication of early believers and the many powerful miracles they performed. But within a few years, infighting and arguments over tiny details of faith and practice tore apart these once-dynamic congregations.

In 1 Corinthians, Paul lectured the believers in Corinth about their sexual immorality (including adultery and incest), their arguments over whether or not Christians could eat meat sacrificed to pagan gods, and the fighting that erupted over one of the most important Christian rituals—the Lord's Supper.

As if these problems weren't bad enough, Christians were also getting upset with each other about the use of such spiritual gifts as prophesy and speaking in tongues, which were common at the time. They wanted to know which gifts were most important (and perhaps, which Christians were most important, too).

Paul tried to defuse their childish competitiveness. "If I speak in the tongues of men and of angels, but have not love. . . . I am nothing," he wrote (1 Cor. 13:1–2), demonstrating that it was not one's gift that was most important but how one used it.

"Love is patient," he continued, spelling out the key characteristics of this most important virtue. "Love is kind. It does not envy, it does not boast, it is not proud" (v. 4).

Paul even argued that love was more important than faith and hope, two virtues that the Bible celebrates throughout its pages.

If it were not for faith, we would not be able to believe God and see his work in our lives. If it were not for hope, we would be unable to apply this life-transforming faith to the challenge of daily life.

Even still, it is love that knits the whole package together in a way that is pleasing to God and helpful to others.

———

God, help me to realize that you care about not only what I do, but why I do it.

The Seasons of Life

There is a time for everything,
and a season for every activity under heaven.

Ecclesiastes 3:1

OUR daughter Lisa, her husband, Chadd, their four boys, and Maggie, their Newfoundland, are living with us for several months. The boys, Justin, Alex, Brady and Dylan, are eight, five, three, and eighteen months.

Chadd and Lisa are building a new house that will be ready in early November, and they have sold their previous home. So, their interim housing is with Nana and Papa.

Steve and I have had some years of grandparenting experience and love the total of seven little ones with whom God has blessed us. We have watched the grandchildren grow and their parents teach and train them.

Now our experience has moved from numerous visits during the year to living together for eight of us. We are getting an up-close and firsthand look at life with young children again.

Steve and I marvel. Our grandsons are wonderful to be around, well-behaved and loving. And they are very busy. We become worn-out just watching them tumble through a day. Their energy seems limitless and their basic needs consume the better part of our daughter's day.

I'd love to be more helpful to Lisa. In fact when the first grandchild was born I imagined that I could handle as many babies as arrived, for any amount of time, no matter the number of their activities. I even thought about getting a van so I could have all of them with me at once.

I have found this to be a fantasy. And I am shocked. I never expected to be too tired to do anything that I wanted to do. I scoffed at the idea of aging in a way that would limit my activities.

But I have found the truth of Ecclesiastes 3:1 not only to be true, but to be freeing. How wonderful of God to give us this verse and the ones that follow to free us from the guilt that seems to accompany some changes in our lives.

I had a season of motherhood when I was the age of my daughters, and it was wonderful. When I look back on those years I am amazed at my own life and how God provided all that I needed for that season.

Seasons allow us to experience God in the differing dimensions of our lives in ways that reveal his wisdom. Because we live in a fallen world, we will age and eventually go to be with him. That process is gradual for most of us and requires merely that we learn to live and enjoy life at a pace that matches our physical aging.

This isn't bad news. Eternity is ahead, and God carries us all the way through on our journey there.

———

Father, thank you for the changing seasons of life and for your presence throughout all of our days, here and in eternity.

Inner Beauty in an Age of Outer Image

Your beauty should not come from outward adornment, such as braided hair and the wearing of gold jewelry and fine clothes. Instead, it should be that of your inner self, the unfading beauty of a gentle and quiet spirit, which is of great worth in God's sight.

1 Peter 3:3–4

OPEN up a magazine, turn on the TV, watch a movie, or glance up at a highway billboard and you will be getting much more than a carefully crafted message designed to sell you the latest high-priced consumer products. You will also be getting a not-so-subtle message about what the ideal woman looks like.

You know the type. She is tall and slender, with curvaceous hips and ample breasts. Her skin is as smooth as porcelain. She has brilliant white teeth, which shine from between lush, lipsticked lips. Her flowing hair cascades over her majestic shoulders. She is decked out in designer duds that look as though they might require an army of maids to keep cleaned and pressed. And she's about twenty-five years old.

This ideal woman beckons to us from commercials for toothpaste,

shampoo, and all the products that promise to help us have a happier, less harried life. Dressed up in spotless clothes and high heels, she tries to sell us jewelry or refrigerators. Or dressed down in a bikini or sexy slacks, she tries to sell us automobiles or beer.

But no matter what she's selling us today, this ideal woman is also promoting the so-called "good life," which is guaranteed to be ours if we buy all the right products.

Ads help sell products, but they also serve as a constant reminder to women of all ages that they just don't measure up to society's lofty standard. For young girls, this destructive message can lead not only to desperate efforts to buy all the right clothes but also more disturbing behaviors such as eating disorders and depression.

Who knows what Peter would have thought of our high-gloss, high-pressure ads? He certainly had a different ideal of womanhood. "Your beauty should not come from outward adornment," he wrote, but from "your inner self, the unfading beauty of a gentle and quiet spirit, which is of great worth in God's sight."

Peter wasn't one who insisted that women remain quiet unless spoken to. His letters counseled men and women to treat one another with love and respect. But such respect doesn't come from outer image. Outward adornments are little more than window dressing. It's the internal characteristics that make us who we really are.

People have tried to outdo each other ever since primitive human tribes made the first bearskin robes. Christians of Peter's day had the same problem, even before advertising helped increase desire and spending.

Incessant advertising certainly makes it more difficult to follow Peter's sage advice. Every day each one of us is bombarded by TV commercials, ads in magazines and newspapers, billboards that line our roads and highways, and flashing come-ons that confront us every time we surf the Internet. Designed to prey on our weaknesses and vulnerabilities, these advertising messages do more than sell us products. They attempt to sell us an entire worldview that claims we are what we wear and what we look like. In these ever-present sales pitches, the people who drive the right cars, buy the right clothes and use the right shampoo and makeup invariably find love and happiness, while those who use Brand X are left high and dry.

Surrounded as we are by such a chorus of consumer messages, it may be hard for us to hear Peter's simple truth that it's what's inside that matters most. But Peter's message may be just the advice we need to survive in our outward-oriented culture.

———

Father, help me focus my energy on inner beauty. Make my soul a beautiful thing that radiates your grace and love outward to those with whom I come in contact.

68

Higher Power

"For my thoughts are not your thoughts,
*neither are your ways my ways," declares the L*ORD*.*
"As the heavens are higher than the earth,
so are my ways higher than your ways
and my thoughts than your thoughts."

Isaiah 55:8–9

WHENEVER travel requires me to take an evening air flight, I make sure I reserve a window seat. That way, I can look out the window into the darkened night and watch cities and towns pass by below.

When the plane takes off the runway, I watch the airport facilities grow smaller. As the plane picks up altitude, I can see cars stopped at traffic lights. Sometimes I can distinguish schools from churches from apartment complexes. It's even more fun when I can see a nighttime baseball game, bright floodlights illuminating the small diamond and the tiny players.

Once the plane has reached its cruising altitude some five miles above the earth, it's much more difficult to pick out many details. Still, I can see the outlines of cities and towns, along with an occasional highway.

The final twenty minutes of a flight once again reveal human civilization's vast scope and technological achievement. I often look out the little window of my plane, amazed at the breadth and diversity of all I see spread out below me. Cities and streets that often look so congested and dirty when seen up close can seem awe-inspiring from a distance. Sometimes I even say to myself, *You know, we human beings are really pretty darn smart!*

But God has a view of human life that's even loftier than the one I enjoy when I'm flying. As God looks down on the entire world from heaven, he has a slightly different perspective on things from mine.

God appreciates much of what humanity has done with the gifts and abilities he has lavished on us. At the same time, he's less excited about some of what he sees.

He created us to live together on the earth and experience some of the love that is at the core of his nature. But too often, competition and strife characterize human affairs—both on the global scale and in our dealings with our neighbors.

God created humans to live in a sense of balance with the natural world. But sadly, our civilizations often plunder the earth and leave portions of it uninhabitable for future generations.

God set the earth in the sky where the sun lit it by day and the moon by night. But now, our own electric lights often blot out the beauty and majesty of God's creation.

There's still much to admire in humanity and in what it has created. But that's not the entire story. God stands above all we do, providing a continual reminder of what true glory is.

———

God, thank you for all of creation. Help me to see beyond this world to the glory and majesty of your nature.

69

A Faith That Transforms

Now faith is being sure of what we hope for and certain of what we do not see. This is what the ancients were commended for.

Hebrews 11:1

WHAT is faith? One man gave this curious response: "Faith is believing in something that you know isn't true."

For some people, faith is something they use as an irrational defense against a cold, cruel world. This kind of faith might help an insomniac get through another sleepless night, but it's not the kind of faith that will transform our lives or please the God who wants his followers to trust him with childlike abandon.

Francis Schaeffer was an influential Christian thinker who lived many years in the Swiss Alps. So when he tried to explain faith in his book, he did so in a way that made sense to him: Suppose you've been out hiking in the mountains when a blizzard sneaks up on you. Just as the snow and wind surround you in a blinding fog, you find yourself on a small rocky ledge unsure of where to go.

If you suddenly get a strange notion in your head that the path back home is a few feet below you and you jump, based on your faith in that notion, this is blind faith. Your faith may be strong, but that doesn't mean you will land safely.

On the other hand, suppose you're sitting on your rock ledge, shivering in the biting cold, and you hear a voice calling out to you. The voice says, "Hello, you can't see me, but I know where you are and I know how you can reach safety. You need to walk to the edge of the ledge and jump. When you land, I will be there to care for you and take you safely home."

In this case, jumping would still require an act of faith, but this wouldn't be a blind leap into the dark. It would be a reasoned faith that the man who called out to you is really there and means what he says.

How can we be sure of something we don't see? How can we have hope in something we can't touch? This is the kind of faith God wants from us. Though we cannot see him, he wants us to trust him. And though we cannot touch him, he desires that we place ourselves in his outstretched arms.

When people claim that God doesn't exist, he instead wants us to believe in him and rely on him. When it looks like life is pointless and meaningless, God wants us to have faith that he is still in control and is working behind the scenes to do his work. And when it seems that we are surrounded by evil and it looks as if the darkness will prevail, God wants us to trust in his promise that good will ultimately prevail.

This is the kind of faith for which God has commended believers throughout the ages. And it is the only kind of faith that will see us safely home.

God, there are times I wish I could touch you or see you face-to-face. But until then, help me to believe and remain faithful.

70

An Audience of One

Be careful not to do your "acts of righteousness" before men, to be seen by them. If you do, you will have no reward from your Father in heaven.

Matthew 6:1

WHENEVER a trash-talking pop singer or self-important movie star bad-mouths God, the American way, motherhood, or apple pie, politicians almost trample each other in their stampede to find the nearest television news crew and declare their undying devotion to all things noble and true.

And at campaign time, when votes are on the line, candidates crawl out of the woodwork to appear at churches, parades, civic events, concerts, and workplaces to portray themselves as ten times more concerned about average guys and gals than their political opponents.

It's not just politicians who like to be seen being good. When billionaire philanthropists give big checks to well-known charities, they make sure photographers are there to capture the act. And when a corporate leader opens a new plant and hires more workers, he invites the local paper to the ribbon-cutting ceremony.

Even some church people can fall prey to the temptation to put performance over substance. In decades past, people who spent Monday through Saturday ignoring fashion would wear their Sunday best to go to church. While there's less emphasis on dress at many contemporary churches, some people still feel an overpowering need to be up front teaching, preaching, singing, praying, or praising the Lord.

There's nothing wrong with doing good things. And there's nothing wrong with being seen doing good—as long as that's not the main reason you're doing it.

Be careful, said Jesus. *If you do things primarily to fill your own hunger for personal affirmation or public approval, that's all the reward you will get.*

"When you give to the needy, do not announce it with trumpets," Jesus said. "When you pray, do not be like the hypocrites, for they love to pray standing in the synagogues and on the street corners to be seen by men" (Matt. 6:2,5).

When we do things merely so others will see us, we short-circuit God's eternal desire that his children would do good deeds for him. If we perform only for the crowd's applause, Jesus had a warning for us: "I tell you the truth, they have received their reward in full" (Matt. 6:5).

One of the most saintly people of recent years was a tiny but tireless woman named Mother Teresa. Born into a wealthy family, she left it all behind to serve the poorest of the poor in the slums of Calcutta, India. Her parents tried to pressure her into finding some other kind of work, but Teresa chose to remain true to her calling, even though it meant being cut off from her family and losing her share of a substantial inheritance.

We've all heard the phrase "upwardly mobile." But Mother Teresa's ministry followed the opposite trajectory: she was wholeheartedly "downwardly mobile." Instead of courting the favor of the famous or the powerful, she sought to do nothing more than to be a servant to impoverished people who tried to survive at the bottom of India's highly stratified socioeconomic ladder. Of course, the people she and her sisters helped were thankful, but Teresa deflected their praise, encouraging them to thank God rather than her.

Naturally, Mother Teresa's work attracted plenty of attention. Reporters from around the world repeatedly tried to interview her, but she typically turned down most of these opportunities.

Some people thought she was crazy, but unlike pop stars and politicians, she knew she wouldn't find her true reward in the glare of the spotlights. Instead, she made her life into a performance intended for an audience of one. And she rested in the assurance that God had accepted her sacrifice and was cheering her on from heaven.

———

Father, help me to do more things for only your eyes and approval.

71

Honoring God's Name

Some trust in chariots and some in horses,
but we trust in the name of the LORD our God.

Psalm 20:7

I STOOD in front of the traveling Vietnam Memorial. Several dozen other people moved quietly along the granite columns filled with names.

Sam Harrell, Doug Johnson, and Paul Martindale—they were all names of young men who had been in helicopter flight school with my first husband, Jack, and all three had been killed in Vietnam.

How fitting to remember these war dead in this simple but profound way. The name of each man who gave his life in Vietnam is etched in stone for all to see.

The mere mention of a person's name can evoke a lifetime of memories in the hearts of those who knew that person. We can see the person in our mind's eye and feel his or her presence.

If our human names carry this much weight, how much more so the name of the Lord? His name not only identifies who he is, but it carries his power in it. That power transcends the limitations of time and space and moves in supernatural ways on our behalf.

In Psalm 20:7 David compared the power of the name of the Lord with the power the military usually relied upon in times of war. In this text an army would have been in sorry shape without chariots and horses, and yet the name of the Lord was even more powerful than those human means.

In the name of the Lord demons are cast out (Matt. 7:22), we offer our prayers and requests (John 14:13), and we are protected from forces that would fell armies (Ps. 20:7).

It is challenging to communicate the importance of God's name in Scripture, but one of God's most declarative statements appears in Exodus 3:14 when Moses asked God his name, and God responded, "I AM WHO I AM." The verb here comes from the Hebrew word *hayah*, which may imply "I am he who is," or "I am he who exists."

The original Hebrew combination of letters that signified the name of God was YHWH. The Israelites considered this word too sacred even to pronounce. When reading God's name, they combined the vowels in the Hebrew word for "My Lord" and the consonants YHWH to form the word *Jehovah*.

In Hebrew names carried great significance and were not mere labels. So the words used for God's name conveyed his divinity and the great importance of who he was.

His name is so powerful for us that the mention of it calls God himself to our aid.

———

Father, we cannot even comprehend the power your name implies. Thank you that we have full access to it and to you.

72

Salt and Light for a Dull and Darkened World

You are the salt of the earth. But if the salt loses its saltiness, how can it be made salty again? It is no longer good for anything, except to be thrown out and trampled by men.

You are the light of the world. A city on a hill cannot be hidden. Neither do people light a lamp and put it under a bowl. Instead they put it on its stand, and it gives light to everyone in the house. In the same way, let your light shine before men, that they may see your good deeds and praise your Father in heaven.

Matthew 5:13–16

SALVATION through Christ is the highest purpose of our entire existence. But life doesn't end there. Instead, coming to know Christ is just the beginning of a new life we live for a higher purpose.

God doesn't give grace solely for our selfish enjoyment. It's not something we should hoard and hide away. Rather, salvation is a divine gift we receive so that we may help give it to others.

Christ explained this concept in terms his listeners could understand. Today, the compound known as sodium chloride is a readily available and inexpensive substance we use to add flavor to our food. But in the time of Christ, salt was a precious commodity that people used to preserve meat and foods. At times in the distant past, they traded an ounce of salt for an ounce of gold. Long ago, people established caravan routes that crossed the ancient world to transport salt from place to place.

Sometimes, as traders were transporting salt across long distances, other substances would adulterate it, or rain or a sudden flood would ruin it. When this happened, it no longer had any value. Its preservative value lost, traders would throw it away.

Today, light is always as near as the closest light switch. Thanks to plentiful electricity and the development of ever-brighter bulbs, people can illuminate their homes, businesses, and ballparks at all hours of the night or day.

But suppose you turn on a light in a closet, then close the door and forget about it. The light is still burning, but nobody can see or benefit from its light.

When Christ told his followers that they were salt and light, he meant that they were supposed to have a transforming impact on the society around them. Like salt, they were to preserve the good in society, preventing it from rotting and going bad. Like light, they were to illuminate the darkness, enabling people to see the truth and follow it.

God's gifts are wonderful things to enjoy, but our enjoyment is not the bottom line. Christ saved us so that we could help him save others. Only when we act as salt and light in our world will we accomplish this urgent assignment.

_____

Father, help me to be salt and light in this needy world.

73

Open That Door

Surely the arm of the LORD is not too short to save,
nor his ear too dull to hear.
But your iniquities have separated you from your God;
your sins have hidden his face from you,
so that he will not hear.

Isaiah 59:1–2

ONE of the most famous paintings of Christ shows him standing in a garden facing a large, wooden door. Jesus is dressed in flowing robes, his long, curly hair cascading over his shoulders. There's a look of eager anticipation in his eyes.

But there's something funny about the door. It has no handle, keyhole, or other means of opening it. That's because the painter was trying to illustrate the message of one of the most powerful verses of the New Testament. In Revelation 3:20, Jesus delivered this loving invitation: "Here I am! I stand at the door and knock. If anyone hears my voice and opens the door, I will come in and eat with him, and he with me."

This may sound like an invitation to a meal, but Jesus has more on his mind here than dinner and dessert. The same man who used terms like *living water* to explain the work of the Holy Spirit also meant more by the word *food* than might seem obvious at first. John, who wrote the Book of Revelation, shows us what Jesus meant in the fourth chapter of his Gospel, where Jesus tells a Samaritan woman, "My food is to do the will of him who sent me and to finish his work." So when Jesus says he will come and eat with us, it probably means he will be sharing more than food with us. It means he will be sharing his life, which will enable us better to do his will.

Jesus wants us to open the door and invite him into our lives, but he's a gentleman. He's not going to barge in if we don't really want him there. We need to ask him in.

The Book of Isaiah explores a similar theme. It describes God's repeated attempts to reach out to the people of Israel. It's a sad and depressing story. Time after time, God rescued the people from their latest blunders. Then, after a period of soul-searching and repentance, the people asked God to forgive them. They rededicated themselves to faith and righteous living, and promised that nothing like that would ever happen again.

But within a few pages or paragraphs, they were up to their old shenanigans once again. They turned their backs on God and experienced the natural consequences of such disobedience.

This goes on for sixty-six chapters. By the time I finish reading Isaiah, I feel a mix of frustration and hope. There's frustration because the book powerfully shows how stupid and mule-headed human beings can be. But there's hope because God keeps trying new things to get our attention once again.

Some people question whether or not God exists, and at least part of their rationale comes from the fact that things on planet Earth never seem to get much better. Sure, technology improves, but human nature stays the same, embroiling the globe in conflict and wars.

But such recurring problems shouldn't be a cause for doubting

God. Rather, we should praise God for his steadfast commitment to us in the face of so much opposition and disobedience.

God's arm isn't short. He isn't deaf to our cries. The problem is us and our repeated preference for our own ways over God's way.

Only when we realize that and open the door to Jesus will we see the face of God in all its glory.

———

Father, please come into my life and make yourself at home in my heart.

f Christ didn't mean the end of sacrifices. Instead, God now
s all of us to live in such ways that our lives are moment-to-
ent "living sacrifices."

ul told us to offer our bodies, but this does not mean that we
oe ritually killed and burned on a smoking altar. Rather, it
s that we should give our lives to God for his use and service.
oerson who does this offers a word of kindness and mercy to
one who needs it. He forgives those who hurt and demean him.
res to others even when he doesn't feel like it or when he would
 have someone give to him. He makes himself available for
use even though his daily schedule is already full of more tasks
e can accomplish.

ay, many churches have become battlegrounds in what some
 have called the "worship wars." Some people prefer to sing
and recite classic Christian statements like the Apostles' Creed.
 prefer singing contemporary praise choruses and keeping
services low-key and informal.

had a different point of view. As he told us, offering ourselves
as living sacrifices is an "act of worship" that pleases God. It
host important kind of worship.

 hung on the cross, Jesus offered up these words to his heav-
ther: "Father, into your hands I commit my spirit" (Luke
God may not require that you and I suffer and die on a cross.
loes require that we offer up our lives to him in worship so
use them for his glory.

, much of the time I think only about what I want and what
ake me happy. But help me develop a different attitude. I want
* to be a living sacrifice to you.*

74

Made Clean in God's Sight

To him who is able to keep you from falling and to present you before
his glorious presence without fault and with great joy—to the only God
our Savior be glory.

Jude 1:24–25

ON one of our adventures to Ireland, Steve and I traveled over
eight miles of rough seas to explore the ancient monastic island of Skellig Michael.

Waves splashed over the side of the boat and drenched us. My
wool hat was flattened to my head and salt stung my chapped lips.
When we stepped onto the rocky hills of Skellig Michael, I was cold
but anxious to get started hiking and exploring. We had about two
hours to wander and climb on this breathtaking island that is home
to monastic ruins dating back as much as fifteen hundred years.

I did the wandering and Steve did the climbing. But wherever either of us went, the ground was muddy. Our hiking boots kept our
feet dry, but the grooved bottoms of the boots were caked with muck.

As soon as we landed back on the mainland, we headed for the nearest pub to try and dry off a little and get some of the junk off our boots. It was a useless endeavor. We were a mess.

We drove back to our bed-and-breakfast, eager for a hot shower and clean clothes. It took a lot of scrubbing to get the salt out of my hair and off my face. The next day I picked the dried mud out of the crevices of my boots with a knife, but my wool cap was a total loss. It was loaded with salt and grime and no amount of scrubbing would save it.

I think of this passage in Jude when I remember how filthy Steve and I were on this adventure. We are all full of filth on the inside. Even when we look our cleanest, our hearts harbor the vestiges of sin. God calls us to be perfect (Matt. 5:48), and no amount of scrubbing on our part will accomplish that perfection. The crevices of our souls, like the crevices on my hiking boots, are full of the mud of life lived in a fallen and dirty world.

Someone has said that the ground at the foot of the cross is level, meaning that we have all sinned and are all filthy. It matters not what sins we have committed. Even those of us with the least amount of filth are as guilty as those with the most. The "knife" that might have been used to "clean" us was used, instead, on Jesus as he hung on the cross.

None of us are clean as we stand before God, resting on our own efforts. But we don't rest on our own efforts. As this verse declares, we rest on him who presents us "without fault."

———

Father, what a miracle that your Son paid our debt for us, and now we are clean before you.

75

A Living Sacr

Therefore, I urge you, brothers, in view of Go bodies as living sacrifices, holy and pleasing spiritual act of worship.

Before the time of Jesus, people who wa so by making the offerings and sacrific Large portions of the Old Testament Bool and Deuteronomy spell out the detailed used to bring an offering or sacrifice to temple.

Jesus both upheld and radically transf ficial system. He visited the temple durin in the Passover meal. But then he himse dying for us and our sins on the cross.

In the seconds before he died, Jesus u ished" (John 19:30). In saying these w had completed the sacrifice God had de

But as Paul pointed out in the passag

76

Wisdom Bigger Than Our Own

When you hear them sound a long blast on the trumpets, have all the people give a loud shout; then the wall of the city will collapse and the people will go up, every man straight in.

Joshua 6:5

WORDS featured in a song in the children's video *Josh and the Big Wall* declare that walking around a wall looks like a pretty dumb idea. Characters in these videos are personified as vegetables and fruit, and the singers in this scene are peas dressed as Canaanite guards with Roman helmets on their heads. They are standing on top of the wall of Jericho and singing down to the Israelites who are portrayed as marching peas and pickles.

Josh, played by a cucumber, and his followers have told the guards that God told them to march around the wall, which would cause it to fall.

The pea-guards are not impressed or worried and tell Josh and his people to go ahead and march all they want. Of course, in the end of the video, the wall comes tumbling down and the pea-guards find themselves tangled in the rubble. They run off in fear and God's forces win the battle.

Whimsical as this children's video seems, it communicates a message: the world often sees the followers of God as unsophisticated and intellectually deficient. Even though we know that the "foolishness of God is wiser than man's wisdom" (1 Cor. 1:25), the people of Jericho didn't know that and many of our contemporaries don't know it either.

A number of years ago I attended a debate between a creationist and an evolutionist. Both men had a string of academic credentials after their names and sounded very convincing. The audience seemed to be filled with people who knew or admired one of the two men. They divided their applause equally between the two debaters.

As we filed out of the auditorium I overheard several people commenting on the stupidity of Christians. It seemed that even the credentials and scholarly presentation of the Christian debater couldn't convince these skeptics.

With all the world's information available to us, we may still seem like the little veggie army marching around Jericho. People who do not know God will probably continue to tell us our "brains are very small," but God's power has overcome the world.

Ultimately, though, the walls of disbelief will fall down and he will reveal himself for who he really is.

————

Father, thank you that your wisdom is greater than any worldly wisdom and that you give us strength to follow you even when criticized.

77

Pathway to Heaven or Highway to Hell?

Enter through the narrow gate. For wide is the gate and broad is the road that leads to destruction, and many enter through it. But small is the gate and narrow the road that leads to life, and only a few find it.

Matthew 7:13–14

Poets, authors, and musicians have incorporated the image of the road into their work for centuries. From John Bunyan's *The Pilgrim's Progress* to the Beatles' "Long and Winding Road," highways and byways have played an important supporting role in art and popular culture.

Jesus used the metaphor of the road, too. But he said only a few people choose the right road in life. The rest are headed full-speed down a big, broad superhighway to hell.

Was Jesus having a bad day or feeling unusually pessimistic when he delivered these sobering comments?

Many people would like to believe that everyone is going to heaven. Well, not everyone; we can take out people like Hitler and

Stalin. And maybe the guy who invented karaoke. All of the others get a free pass to heaven, in our minds, thanks to their good works, or because we like them, or because we can't bear the thought of their going to hell.

Jesus doesn't like the thought of anyone going to hell, either. He came to earth and gave his life on the cross so that wouldn't have to happen. But as he said in the passage above, there are basically two ways to go in life, and most people choose the wrong one.

How could this be the case if God loves everyone? Theologians have wrestled with this question for centuries. Many conclude that the fact that God loves all of us doesn't mean all of us will love him back.

Jesus explained some of this in his parable of the sower and the seed (Matt. 13). A farmer went out one day to sow some seed. Some of the seed fell on the path where the birds came and ate it. Some fell on bad soil where it started growing, then died off. Some fell in the thorns, which choked its growth. And some fell on fertile soil, where it took root and produced a bumper crop.

Jesus told that parable to a large crowd of people, but later, he gave a more detailed explanation to his disciples. The seed, he said, represents the message of the kingdom. "When anyone hears the message about the kingdom and does not understand it the evil one comes and snatches away what was sown in his heart," said Jesus. "This is the seed sown along the path. The one who received the seed that fell on the rocky places is the man who hears the word and at once receives it with joy. But since he has no root, he lasts only a short time. When trouble or persecution comes because of the word he quickly falls away."

Jesus never explained his comments about the two roads, but if he had, it might have gone something like this: Many people get in their cars and go out for a drive. Some have no clear destination in mind and spend their lives wandering throughout the world. Others know where they would like to go but get lost or distracted along the way. Only a few people make it to their ultimate destination.

This may not be a very "positive" message. You won't see Jesus' comments about the narrow road on a colorful greeting card. But not everything God says makes us happy. It needs only to be true.

———

God, help me stay on the narrow path to you and not get sidetracked on the wide way.

78

Dancing Again

You turned my wailing into dancing;
you removed my sackcloth and clothed me with joy.

Psalm 30:11

I (LOIS) grew up about thirty miles south of Philadelphia, the location of the original *American Bandstand* TV show. The dances we saw on *Bandstand* one week showed up on our school dance floor the next week.

Three years out of high school I married one of the best dancers in the class, Jack Mowday, and we clicked our heels together for the next thirteen years.

Then in December of 1979, the dancing stopped. Our daughters Lisa and Lara and I got Jack a ride in a hot-air balloon as a Christmas present. Two of his close friends and business associates, Glenn Berg and Rick Rhine, as well as a balloon operator went along with him.

The girls and I, along with Glenn's wife, Gail, and Rick's fiancée, Kathy, rode in our station wagon and followed the balloon in flight. It was a beautiful day and the guys waved happily as they sailed along.

We lost sight of the balloon behind some trees and when it reappeared, a blaze was growing out of the side of the basket. We knew immediately that the men and the pilot were in terrible trouble as the flames licked up over the edge of the basket and into the small passenger space.

All four people were killed that day, and my life changed forever. But God carried us in miraculous ways.

The truth of his promises became a reality for me and my daughters, and we experienced grace far beyond our imagination. While pain and loneliness were sometimes consuming, so was the peace of God. I learned that peace and pain coexist and breathe hope into the darkest of nights.

But even when I felt God's arms of love embrace me, I doubted that I would ever be truly happy again, and I was sure that my spirit would never be able to dance with the joy I'd known when Jack was alive.

One of my great comforts during those early days of grief came from copying verses on index cards and carrying them with me. I'd read them when waiting in the car for the girls to get out of school or at a dentist's office. Sometimes the words would seem flat, and God would seem distant. Nights were the most difficult times; the hours dragged until the sun shone again.

But then those dark times grew less frequent. The words of the verses touched me in a healing way and my heart felt full again. My spirit danced.

Many of the verses I wrote on these cards came from the Psalms. The language and poetry of the Psalms lend themselves to creating a place of peace in the reader's heart. I also love to read the Psalms in the King James Version of the Bible, but you may find more comfort in another version.

A few of my favorite verses are:

Psalm 4:8—"I will lie down and sleep in peace, for you alone, O Lord, make me dwell in safety."

Psalm 32:7—"Thou art my hiding place: thou shalt preserve me from trouble: thou shalt compass me about with songs of deliverance."

Psalm 34:18—"The Lord is nigh unto them that are of a broken heart . . ."

Psalm 34: 4—"I sought the Lord, and he heard me, and delivered me from all my fears."

I don't live down the road from *American Bandstand* anymore, and I don't dance anywhere but in my family room on very rare occasions. But I *can* dance. The wailing has ended, the sackcloth of grief is gone and he has "clothed me with joy."

Father, when pain is great we sometimes despair. How faithful you are to heal our wounds and bring our spirits back to places of joy.

79

The Two Main Things

Love the Lord your God with all your heart and with all your soul and with all your mind and with all your strength. . . . "Love your neighbor as yourself." There is no commandment greater than these.

Mark 12:30–31

As Jesus walked the earth teaching about the kingdom of God and caring for the people he met, he attracted all kinds of followers and curious onlookers.

His disciples were his inner circle. They ate, walked, and lived with their master, and heard more of his lessons than anyone.

At times, Jesus attracted people the Bible calls "the crowds." Whenever he performed a startling miracle or fed five thousand with some loaves of bread and a few fish, people followed him as they would a traveling sideshow, waiting to see what kinds of new and exciting things he would do next.

A third group of people who kept track of Jesus were the Jewish religious leaders, who were called teachers of the law, Pharisees, Saducees, and other terms.

It was sometimes hard to figure out what members of this group thought about Jesus. Some of them listened closely to what he said because they believed he might be the fulfillment of ancient prophecies about the coming Messiah. Others dismissed most of what he said because they didn't like how he was demolishing their entrenched religious traditions.

In Mark 12, Jesus had a series of conversations with various groups of Jewish leaders. After skillfully answering a number of tough theological questions, Jesus faced yet another. A teacher of the Law asked, "Of all the commandments, which is the most important?" (v. 28)

This is the kind of question most theologians could spend their lives debating. Their deliberations might even yield a series of arcane books that spend as much time avoiding the question as answering it.

But Jesus responded in a way that was simple and direct. "Love the Lord your God with all your heart and with all your soul and with all your mind and with all your strength. The second is this: 'Love your neighbor as yourself.' There is no commandment greater than these."

The man who asked the question was impressed with Jesus' answer and concluded that such love was more important than even sacrifices. At the end of their talk, Jesus told him, "You are not far from the kingdom of God" (Mark 12:34).

In our day, things seem so complex. There are so many conflicting voices vying for our attention and allegiance. But Jesus says our goals in life are really straightforward.

Of course, knowing what we need to do doesn't necessarily mean we'll always do it, but at least we know what our goal is. If we focus on loving God and loving our neighbor, everything else will fall into place.

———

Father, help me love you and my neighbor in everything I do.

80

A Crying God

Jesus wept.

John 11:35

This shortest verse in the entire Bible reveals one of the most profound truths of the Christian faith: that our God is not uncaring and aloof from our problems but can understand and feel our pain.

I'm the kind of person who cries when I see someone else crying. Even movie and TV tears can have me reaching for tissues.

Why do I feel such emotion for people I don't even know? Because I have had my share of suffering, hurt, and loss, and I can imagine how they feel.

That's part of why I find this verse in John's Gospel so powerful. John 11 tells us that Lazarus and his two sisters, Mary and Martha, were close friends and devoted followers of Jesus. One day the two sisters came to Jesus with troubling news: Lazarus was gravely ill. By the time Jesus and his disciples returned to Bethany, Lazarus was dead.

Mary was brokenhearted and grieved for her lost brother. Others who had known him wept along with her. Jesus joined in with them, shedding his own tears of sorrow for a beloved old friend.

The passage doesn't tell us how long Jesus cried or give us any details about the sorrow that touched his heart. It simply says: "Jesus wept." Then Jesus called: "Lazarus, come out!" Lazarus emerged from his tomb, his smelly grave clothes dangling from his face, hands, and feet.

Over the centuries, Christians have cherished this amazing passage, which demonstrates Jesus' power over life and death. But by focusing on the dramatic miracle of Lazarus's resurrection, have we overlooked the importance of Jesus' tears?

The gods of most world religions are too removed from the common concerns of human life to feel our pain or shed a tear. Muhammad is commonly portrayed as a brave warrior, not a sorrowing soul. Statues of Buddha look stone-faced and stoic. Some Hindu gods are angry and vengeful.

Jesus is different. Out of love for us he left his Father in heaven and became a human being so he could reach us right where we were.

For more than thirty years, he walked this earth, tasting the joys and tragedies of ordinary life. In time his deep love would lead him to pay the ultimate price—sacrificing his own life on the cross in order to save us from our sin.

Jesus' tears show that he feels as we do.

As with our own tears, his came only after he could no long contain the swelling waves of sorrow. The droplets that spilled down his face reveal that he can understand our broken dreams, our dashed hopes, and the many pains that come from dealing with life and loss.

Jesus understands, and the Savior who raised Lazarus will someday raise us.

———

God, thank you for sharing the pain I often feel in this life. May sorrow and tears cleanse my heart and deepen my love.

Serving Them Serves Christ

For I was hungry and you gave me something to eat, I was thirsty and you gave me something to drink, I was a stranger and you invited me in, I needed clothes and you clothed me, I was sick and you looked after me, I was in prison and you came to visit me.

Matthew 25:35–36

Jesus spent thirty years preparing for his three years of ministry. His "final exam" was to undergo an intense forty-day period of testing and tempting by the devil in the desert.

After he passed this grueling test, Jesus went to the synagogue in Nazareth and delivered these stunning lines from the prophet Isaiah:

> "The Spirit of the Lord is on me,
> because he has anointed me
> to preach good news to the poor.
> He has sent me to proclaim freedom for the prisoners
> and recovery of sight for the blind,
> to release the oppressed,
> to proclaim the year of the Lord's favor."

(Luke 4:18–19; see Isaiah 61:1)

From that day on, Jesus traveled throughout the countryside, healing the sick, caring for the poor, exorcising demons from the possessed, and preaching the gospel of salvation.

Jesus' words are some of the most beautiful and powerful ones ever spoken, but his ministry was much more than a matter of words. As he continually demonstrated, serving God requires an active, hands-on response to people's pains and problems.

He told us as much in the passage from Matthew. It shows Jesus sitting on a throne of judgment, dividing all of humanity into two groups: the sheep and the goats.

The sheep are those people who did the things Jesus described in verses 35–36. The goats are those people who did not do these things.

But the sheep wondered when they had performed these ministries. Jesus' answer was clear and unmistakable: "I tell you the truth, whatever you did for one of the least of these brothers of mine, you did for me" (v. 40).

In other words, when we feed the hungry, give water to the thirsty, show hospitality to the stranger, clothe those who are naked, and visit those in prison, we are actually doing these things to Jesus.

He didn't explain exactly how this works. This is one of the many mysteries of the faith. But in his words and in his actions, Jesus demonstrated the eternal importance of putting our faith into action. Whether or not we do so is our "final exam."

————

Father, help me reach out to those in need, for in doing so I am ministering to your Son.

God Protects Us

You are my hiding place;
you will protect me from trouble
and surround me with songs of deliverance.

Psalm 32:7

OUR train pulled into the station at Haarlem, The Netherlands, and I couldn't wait to get to the watch shop that had belonged to the family of Corrie Ten Boom. Corrie's family hid Jews in their home during the Nazi occupation of Holland, and she went on to be a famous Christian speaker and writer. The current owners give tours of the living quarters located above the shop.

"There it is!" I pointed and sprinted off ahead of Steve.

On this sunny June day there was no evidence of the dark time in Holland's history when the sound of gestapo boots echoed off the cobbled streets. The Ten Boom watch shop is now a jewelry store on the corner of a bustling tourist thoroughfare. Flowers bloom brightly and children laugh and play without fear.

But Steve and I remembered images from the movie about Corrie's life, *The Hiding Place,* and we reverently walked up the narrow stairs to the living quarters. Much of the Ten Boom's family furniture was still in place.

It was easy to picture the family and their Jewish guests sitting around the dining room table, alert for the sound of the gestapo, but sharing food and conversation like any group of friends would do.

On the next level up we saw Corrie's bedroom and the famous concealed "closet" that safely hid a whole family of Jews. Our guide told of the day that the gestapo took Corrie and her family to a concentration camp.

One would think that after her arrest Corrie might have expressed disappointment in God, since the hiding place led to her own imprisonment. But no. This valiant lady maintained an encouraging spirit while in the camp and became an example to all who know her story that God's safety follows us everywhere . . . even to and beyond the grave.

When the Lord is our hiding place, we are safe no matter what happens. Oh, we may suffer or even die, but our souls are safely carried into his presence in heaven.

And we can experience the powerful presence of God the same way that Corrie did in the prison camp. Our circumstances may be truly threatening, but inside we feel the peace of God that passes all understanding (Phil. 4:7). We are safe.

If our view of God demands that our circumstances be pleasant, we will miss the blessing of feeling safe in the midst of danger. Corrie Ten Boom knew that her own "hiding place" was in God's hands— so is ours.

———

Father, thank you for the strength you gave to Corrie Ten Boom and for her testimony of faith. Grant me strength, too.

83

The Grace That Saves Us

Let your conversation be always full of grace, seasoned with salt, so that you may know how to answer everyone.

Colossians 4:6

ONE of our dear friends heads an international Christian ministry. He and his wife have lived in Europe for more than twenty years.

We met them for dinner while Steve and I were in London a few years ago, and I asked him what he thought Christians in America needed most. This man travels around the world several times a year, so his perspective embraces more of a global view of Christianity than ours does.

Without hesitation he said, "Grace."

Wow! A quick and concise answer.

He went on to explain that he grieved over the petty arguments he witnessed so much of the time when visiting with believers in the United States. He saw the lost condition of much of the world as more important than many of the "in-house" differences we squabbled about.

I was reminded of many cutting words Steve endured when he worked as the religion editor at a Colorado newspaper. Most of these hurtful remarks came from Christians who were critical of him for covering religion stories in an impartial way. And lest I be ungracious myself, let me confess that I have been the queen of sarcasm on many occasions.

Paul called us to speak the truth in love (Eph. 4:15) and Solomon told us that iron sharpens iron (Prov. 27:17), but I do think the "evil one" wreaks havoc among believers when he tempts us to emphasize judgmental words instead of gracious interaction.

One of the most gracious people I know is my friend Marian. She is a sincerely kind person who always gives people the benefit of the doubt. I have been with her and seen her words and manner turn a potential confrontation into a friendly encounter.

A few years ago we were in a grocery store checkout lane when a woman butted in front of Marian. I couldn't believe it, and I was ready to tell this woman to step to the rear. Before I could say a word, Marian smiled at her and stepped back to let her in. "Do you live around here?" Marian asked.

The woman looked surprised but answered. A few more gracious comments from Marian had this woman smiling and talking like they were old friends.

I don't know if God will ever use that brief encounter to bring that woman to a knowledge of Jesus (if she didn't know him already), but I do know that Marian's attitude reflected a light that drew the woman in; it reflected the grace that God gives each of us.

Father, make us all more aware of how we communicate. Help us season our conversations with as much grace as salt.

84

No Whining Please

The LORD said to Joshua, "Stand up! What are you doing down on your face?"

Joshua 7:10

THE Israelites had conquered Jericho and Joshua's "fame spread throughout the land" (Josh. 6:27). But Achan disobeyed God's order. He took some of the things that God had told the Israelites to leave alone.

God's anger "burned against Israel" (Josh. 7:1) and they lost their next battle, suffering the death of some three thousand men. Joshua tore his clothes and fell down on the ground.

The next few verses (Josh. 7:7–9) record Joshua's lament to God. He asked God why he had brought them to this side of the Jordan only for the enemy to defeat them.

Then in verse 10 we have God's response: "Stand up! What are you doing down on your face?"

There Joshua was in front of God the Most High, whining about circumstances, albeit it grave circumstances.

When my behavior resembles Joshua's I find myself paralyzed. I fuss about conditions that don't seem to be my fault. "Why am I so overtired, God? Why did you let me take on so many responsibilities that I can't complete without burning out? Why do you want me to do so much?" Whine, whine, whine.

Then I remember this verse. I love it.

"Stand up!"

"What! Me? But I'm a mess and I'm tired and I need comfort."

"What are you doing down on your face?"

"I'm crying out in front of you, God. Can't I do that?"

And then I can almost see him smile. Of course I can cry in front of God, be honest about my feelings, go to him for comfort.

But sometimes I behave like a spoiled child. I have made some poor choices and had to live in the wake of their consequences. I want a quick fix, a big hug. And instead God draws me up short out of my pity and I face reality.

His words have the power to change my whining to repentance. I know that God has a lot to say about balance and nurture of the soul. Jesus went away by himself to pray (Matt. 14:23), and I don't do that when I am overly busy. I neglect the very thing that gives me life. I don't have time for refreshment from God, so I go to him and complain about all I have to do.

Standing up and looking in the mirror works wonders. I no longer maintain the posture of a victim but come before my Father and ask his forgiveness. Then I decide what I need to do to remedy my situation.

Sometimes the solution is painful. I may have to reevaluate commitments and alter my schedule. I need to pay attention to whatever it is that I have done to render me helpless on the floor.

Then I experience God's forgiveness and blessing. Then I stand up, to his glory.

———

Father, forgive me when I sit in self-pity. Thank you for strong words that change me.

85

The Best Is Yet to Come

No eye has seen,
no ear has heard,
no mind has conceived
what God has prepared for those who love him.

1 Corinthians 2:9

My mother and I went on a trip to Hawaii the summer before my senior year in high school. In those days, Hawaii was a far-off destination reached after a ten-hour plane ride from the West Coast in a noisy propeller plane.

My father didn't want to go but gave this trip to me and my mom as a generous gift. I didn't know a single person who had been to Hawaii, so my daydreams about it were conjured up from movies or magazine pictures I'd seen. I couldn't wait to sit on the beach at Waikiki and imagined its delights for months prior to our departure.

We arrived in Honolulu on a sunny morning in June, and I headed for the beach the minute I unpacked my suitcase. It was beyond my wildest imagination. Diamond Head rose majestically in the distance and the water sparkled with sunlight dancing off the coral reefs below the surface.

Hawaiian music drifted from the stage of the outdoor patio café and breezes rustled palm branches. In those days before Waikiki became a crowded tourist destination, it was idyllic. There were no crowds, the pace of life was slow, the people unhurried in their interactions with visitors, and the natural beauty a visual feast.

God tells us that he has something far richer and deeper to enjoy than anything we can even attempt to comprehend. And this precious gift to us is not limited to the afterlife but begins when we invite Jesus into our hearts.

Though we cannot experience all God has for us this side of heaven, when we are living in deep communion with the Holy Spirit we have a taste of what this verse offers.

I had underestimated the beauty of Hawaii before I arrived there. How much more do we all underestimate what heaven will be like? And even though this verse tells us that we won't be able to imagine what God has planned for us, it is often comforting to allow our minds to wander to the heavens.

There is a saying: "You're so heavenly minded, you're no earthly good." I think we are so earthly minded that we are no heavenly good. We don't enjoy the reality of eternal life in paradise with God forever. We are often so practical and focused on earthly cares that we miss the wonderful anticipation of heaven.

Part of our lack of anticipation is understandable given that death stands between us and heaven. But God has overcome death.

Paradise is actually easier to reach than Hawaii! Believing faith in Christ opens the gates of heaven to us. We have only to think about a place of peace and beauty to sense a longing for heaven.

I was raised in the city but now enjoy walks near our home in the Colorado countryside. The sounds of birds and running brooks replace the noise of urban life. The beauty is natural, not manufactured. Just being outside gives me a glimpse of heaven. And to think that God's wonders here are minimal compared to what he has in store for us in heaven.

———

Father, set our minds free to enjoy all you have for us, today and in the future. Season our earthly sorrow with the joy of knowing you and anticipating being with you eternally.

86

Can God Really Restore Me?

He lifted me out of the slimy pit,
out of the mud and mire;
he set my feet on a rock
and gave me a firm place to stand.

Psalm 40:2

I BECAME a widow when I was thirty-four years old. Since I had married when I was not quite twenty-one, I had no experience as a single adult in the Christian world.

A dear girlfriend warned me about my outgoing behavior and how it could get me into trouble. She told me that a lot of men, married and single, would think that I was flirting with them.

I dismissed her warning with a laugh. Then her words proved to be true. It became evident that some men were more than willing to relieve my loneliness and to excuse immoral behavior with a belief that God "understood."

I stopped hugging men I didn't know well and prayed for a spirit of discernment about my own motives in relationships. About the same time, I started speaking at women's conferences and retreats. Because the women I met were anonymous to me they openly shared their stories.

I was shocked to hear how many Christian women and men were involved in sexual entanglements. The mud and the mire seemed impossible for many to avoid. So many times I heard the words, "God can never forgive me. I have messed up my whole life. I will never be restored again."

In Psalm 40 we read one of the many laments of David, and we have good reason to be encouraged. David's sins were many, and yet God restored him.

I have had so many conversations with women who find themselves in a pit they never anticipated. Their lives have become so entwined with wrongdoing that they see no way to unravel the mess.

But God's power working in their lives can bring them back up out of that pit. They, like David, will suffer consequences for their sins, but also like David, they will be able to praise God for turning their lives around.

How does he do that?

It is really beyond our ability to comprehend the love of God that cleanses us of our sins by the death of his Son on the cross. The cross is the scalpel that cuts out the disease in all of us and replaces it with the healing touch of God.

When we admit our faults, turn from them, and ask God to forgive us, we find ourselves able to make wise choices as never before. We will still struggle, but we will be standing on a firm foundation.

It isn't an easy transition but it is possible, and it is worth the effort. We can embrace the power to see ourselves from God's perspective: as forgiven and loved.

———

Father, protect us from the dangers of the many pitfalls in life that can cause us to sin against you.

87

Contrary to Culture

Do not conform any longer to the pattern of this world, but be transformed by the renewing of your mind. Then you will be able to test and approve what God's will is—his good, pleasing and perfect will.

Romans 12:2

THIS verse expresses two truths that can absolutely revolutionize the life of the believer who grasps them: we can be changed so much that we are actually transformed, and as a result, we can discern God's will.

The first part of this verse confronts us with "the pattern of this world." Certainly one of the glaring realities of our world today is the pluralism that insists any belief is equal to any other belief. Because of this acceptance of all things as true, the establishment of moral absolutes seems too rigid for our culture to tolerate.

The "pattern" of ever-growing self-actualization has elevated individualism to a place of honor in the ranks of desirable human characteristics. As long as any individual's beliefs do not hurt others, society considers them valid and acceptable. There is no common measure of what is true and what is false, allowing a multitude of philosophies and doctrines to coexist.

The problem with this attitude for the Christian is that the claims of Christ render *judgment*—an appalling word in a world that values personal prerogative above all else.

The pattern of today's world insists on multiple views of a greater power that often resembles God, but God as the loving grandfather in the sky. We as believers in the powerful God of Scripture must wrestle with this tempting image and embrace God as we know his Word reveals him. And we can do that because the amazing characteristic of God that coexists with judgment is grace.

Grace, most dramatically displayed in the cross, is what beckons our thoughts toward renewal—toward a "renewed mind." The verb *renew* comes from a Greek word that means to "remember again," as in thinking back to the moment we understood and accepted the gospel. It is the comprehension of God's grace and mercy that transforms our thinking from self-centered to Christ-centered.

The very fact that we can change our minds while living in an environment that so counters Christianity is a powerful and exciting truth. And the bonus that transformed thinking brings is to be able to "test and approve" what the will of God is.

We can navigate our lives in ways that give discernment, think in ways that are informed by the Holy Spirit, and live renewed, transformed by God's power operating in our lives.

This kind of change doesn't happen quickly. There is no formula that assures immediate success. It requires the discipline of continually going to God's Word, reflecting, seeking counsel, and interacting with God and the Holy Spirit through prayer.

———

Father, thank you for access to changed thinking that transforms us into a closer reflection of your Son. Help us to be gracious to others who think differently.

88

Running from God

But Jonah ran away from the LORD.

Jonah 1:3

ONLY four chapters long, the Book of Jonah is one of the short-est in the Old Testament. But it packs a wallop. Jonah's story is one of the most cinematic of the Bible, and it could easily serve as the plot for an action-packed movie.

Jonah's life is a memorable one, even for people who last heard about it in Sunday school decades ago. The book opens with God calling Jonah to serve as a foreign missionary to the wicked city of Nineveh. Jonah heard God's call, then turned and ran away as fast as he could.

He couldn't outrun God, though. Jonah boarded a ship, but God sent violent storms that caused the veteran sailors to take notice. The sailors cast lots to see who might be responsible for the storms and the lot fell to Jonah, whom they reluctantly threw overboard.

Once he was off the ship, the seas calmed. But things were just get-ting exciting for Jonah. God sent a great fish to swallow him. They say there are no atheists in foxholes or fish bellies, and sure enough, Jonah prayed to God once he was imprisoned in the stomach of the whale.

"When my life was ebbing away, / I remembered you, LORD," said Jonah (Jon. 2:7), whom the fish spit up on a beach.

The call of God came a second time: "Go to the great city of Nineveh and proclaim to it the message I give you" (Jon. 3:2). This time Jonah didn't argue. He obeyed God's call.

Billy Graham would like to have had more evangelistic rallies that were as successful as Jonah's crusade in Nineveh. The people of the city believed God's words, declared a fast, and put on sackcloth as a sign of their repentance.

Their response so impressed God that he decided not to destroy the city as he had promised. But this made Jonah mad. He wanted God to zap the once-wicked city. Jonah was so upset that he even asked God to take his life.

God didn't zap Nineveh—or Jonah. Instead, he tried to show Jonah that he cared for those people and would rather see them repent than go to their deaths. "Should I not be concerned about that great city?" God asked (Jon. 4:11).

The Jonah story contains plenty of stunning plot twists and special effects, but stripped of all these elements, it remains a classic story of God's love for humanity, even when we try to thwart his purposes.

God may not call you to preach to a wicked city, and he may not send a big fish to eat you if you disobey. But think about how much better things would go if you did what he asked the first time!

Father, I want to serve you. Help me hear and obey your call on my life.

89

Down but Not Out

We are hard pressed on every side, but not crushed; perplexed, but not in despair.

2 Corinthians 4:8

WOULDN'T it be a pleasant world if we were never "hard pressed" or "perplexed"? Living in and with our unpleasant circumstances can be so tiresome, so frustrating, so constant.

We are weary from the drain of enduring difficulties. No matter what we do, life continues to present one challenge after another. Is it possible that we are missing the means to alleviate stress and pain . . . or are we focusing on the wrong goal?

What was the apostle Paul pursuing in this letter to the Corinthians? The verses that surround 2 Corinthians 4:8 tell us that he didn't seem intent on getting out of the places that caused pressure or perplexity.

Rather he had comprehended that there was a darkness in the world and when he found himself in the middle of it, he had a choice: to fret about the darkness or to reflect the light that life with Jesus breeds.

But how does that work? How do we, still living in the midst of spiritual darkness that disrupts our peace, shine? How do we suffer

as Paul did but not slide down the spiral of negativity that leads to despair?

First, we can take heart that one of the greatest of Scripture's authors lived a life of continual hardship and still penned the words of this verse. The tone Paul used was not one of complaining but one of encouragement. He was telling the Corinthians that he endured persecution for the sake of others, like the people of Corinth, so that they may know Jesus.

Second, we see that Paul had an ability to withstand difficulty with an attitude that preserved his emotional well-being. That ability came from his relationship with Jesus.

Since we have a relationship with Jesus, we, too, can sustain emotional health in the midst of trying times. It is a supernatural reality that we cannot learn or achieve by performance. We comprehend it by focusing on this relationship with God through his Son instead of focusing on alleviating hardship.

Third, we do not resign ourselves to misery and become martyred victims. We choose to believe that Jesus comes into our lives and infuses our thinking, feeling, and volition in ways that allow for a truly overcoming view of the circumstances of our lives.

We don't have to be happy that we suffer, but we can experience the peace of God in the midst of pain.

We, like Paul, point to Jesus when others ask how we can endure suffering and keep going. We don't take credit for exceptional ability. Job is a leading member of the suffering hall of fame (see reading number thirty-nine). But we don't have to look that far back in time for examples of endurance and faith in the midst of suffering. Today and every day around the world, thousands of Christians are suffering for their faith. During the 1990s, the U.S. State Department reported that persecution of Christians is a routine occurrence in more than 70 countries around the world.

Voice of the Martyrs, a ministry in Bartlesville, Oklahoma, is one of many groups that track down reports of persecuted believers worldwide and encourage Americans to pray for them. Some of the reports, like one that detailed the 2002 massacre of a Pakistani pastor and members of his flock, are shocking. But there's another side of the persecution coin. As has been the case for centuries, the blood of the martyrs is the fuel for the growth of the church. And in Pakistan and other countries, persecuted Christians are standing firm by living out their faith and passing it on to others. In many of the countries where persecution is worst, the church is growing at a rapid rate.

And we are not shocked that darkness touches us. We understand that darkness is here because of rebellion against God and that the Light that overcomes the darkness is ours to embrace. It is in Jesus.

———

Father, please give us your comfort in trying times, and allow us to experience your peace.

90

A Ready Resource

*I have hidden your word in my heart
that I might not sin against you.*

Psalm 119:11

In the early days of my Christian life I memorized a lot of Scripture. I have to admit that I am much less diligent in memorizing than I used to be, but I am also often amazed at the words of Scripture that come to mind.

These words are reminders of God's love, commands, promises, and wisdom. They pop into my thoughts and redirect them or suggest a new way to consider a problem.

Their power is surprising. Considering them can actually prompt me to more godly action.

Proverbs 4:23 says to "guard your heart, / for it is the wellspring of life." One of the meanings of the Hebrew word for "wellspring" is "starting point."

Our hearts are the starting points of life. Healthy hearts are essential for life to go on, and that health applies to our spiritual well-being as well as our physical.

We know that sin damages our relationship with God. It comes in and works its darkness, drawing us away from the Father and deceiving us. Sin is powerful. Counterfeit light often cloaks its darkness and lures us into thinking that we are in God's will when we are not.

The Word of God is more powerful than sin. It protects us from all manner of evil and directs us in the ways that we should live. We have this magnificent resource right at our fingertips. It is most likely that anyone reading this book has a Bible. In fact, most of us have many copies and versions of the Bible.

But life's temptations often present themselves when our Bibles are not at hand. Suppose our hearts are not spiritually healthy. Suppose that at the very place from which all life begins we are weak. How will we know what God wants us to do when facing a confusing choice? How will we even be able to discern whether what crosses our path is from God or not?

The answers are in his Word, and there are many ways to study that Word. We hear it in sermons, read it when preparing for Bible studies, listen to it on the radio, meditate on it during times of devotion.

But one of the most powerful ways to maintain access to the Word of God is to memorize it. When it resides in our hearts it sits ready to be called forth at a moment's notice. We don't have to find a Bible and then go to a concordance to locate Scripture to answer our questions. God's Word is in us and fills our hearts with his love and wisdom.

———

Father, help us to visit again the discipline of memorization of your Word. We thank you for its ready access and realize, too, that the safest place for your Word is "hidden" in our hearts.

91

Branches of Christ's Vine

I am the vine; you are the branches. If a man remains in me and I in him, he will bear much fruit; apart from me you can do nothing.

John 15:5

IT had been an amazing three years. Jesus had emerged, seemingly out of nowhere, to preach the message of God's kingdom. He had called twelve men to follow him and be his disciples, and this small band had walked alongside Christ, listening as he taught and watching in amazement as he performed many miracles.

Now their time together was growing short. Jesus had to die, and he tried to explain this to his disciples. He wouldn't be with them any longer, at least not physically, but he would be with them supernaturally to show them the way to the Father.

His lecture met with little success. His disciples didn't understand why he had to die and leave them. "Lord, why can't I follow you now?" asked Peter (John 13:37), who boldly claimed he would lay his life down for Jesus. Thomas was equally puzzled. "Lord, we don't know where you are going, so how can we know the way?" (John 14:5)

Amidst much sorrow and confusion, Jesus carefully explained his mission on the cross, his resurrection, and how the Holy Spirit would be a constant presence in the disciples' lives, teaching them about the ways of God.

Jesus then used a simple illustration to help clear things up. Drawing an agricultural analogy that he was sure the disciples would grasp, he said, "I am the true vine" (John 15:1).

This seemed to make some sense, so he continued his lesson. God is a grand Gardener, he told them, who trims his vines to get rid of the dead and unproductive branches. "If a man remains in me and I in him, he will bear much fruit," said Jesus.

The darkness of incomprehension began to lift, so Jesus explained further. "No branch can bear fruit by itself; it must remain in the vine. . . . If anyone does not remain in me, he is like a branch that is thrown away and withers" (John 15:4, 6).

Jesus was telling his disciples that the message he brought wasn't a series of rules and regulations, but a living, supernatural relationship with God.

Sometimes we are like Jesus' disciples. We just don't get what he is saying. But as long as we cling to him, we will have life and produce much fruit.

———

Father, help me remain connected to you and live a fruitful life.

92

Testing the Spirits

Dear friends, do not believe every spirit, but test the spirits to see whether they are from God, because many false prophets have gone out into the world.

1 John 4:1

THE attractive nine-thousand-square-foot mansion was located in the ritzy Rancho Santa Fe area north of San Diego. It had a manicured lawn and gardens full of colorful, blooming flowers.

But inside, a grisly scene greeted San Diego sheriffs. There, thirty-nine bodies in varying states of decomposition were laid out on simple bunk beds.

The victims were eighteen men and twenty-one women. Their ages varied from twenty-six to seventy-two, but there was no variation in the way they had died. Each victim wore black pants, black shirts, and new black Nike gym shoes. Purple cloths covered their faces and torsos. And to make things easier for those who found them, each body had identification papers nearby.

The grand master bedroom held a body, too. It was the corpse of the unusual group's spiritual leader. His legal name was Marshall

Herff Applewhite, but he went by the nicknames "Do" and "Bo" from the "Bo Peep" nursery rhyme.

Applewhite had promised his followers that they would reach a "level above human" if only they would shed their "containers" (or bodies) and rendezvous with a spaceship waiting for them behind the Hale-Bopp comet. "Planet Earth is about to be recycled," said Applewhite in a videotaped message delivered in his clipped, robotic-sounding voice. "Your only chance to survive—leave with us."

Each victim left a packed suitcase and a farewell statement. "I look very forward to this next major step of ours," said one, "shedding these creatures . . . (and) moving on to the next evolutionary level."

Another said, "I don't have any choice but to go for it, because I've been on this planet for thirty-one years, and there's nothing here for me."[1]

Unfortunately, the tragedy of Heaven's Gate is only one of numerous deaths related to cults of recent years. In April 1993, men, women, and children who followed a man named David Koresh and lived in his Branch Davidian compound near Waco, Texas, died when the place went up in flames. And in March 1995, a Japanese group named Aum Shinri Kyo released the nerve gas sarin into the Tokyo subway system during morning rush hour, killing twelve people and making more than five thousand ill.

It was because of false prophets like these that Jesus commanded his followers through the apostle John to "test the spirits." Not everyone who comes preaching a message of hope and salvation means well. Satan, the father of lies, has deceived many spiritual leaders and those who follow them as well, even if they don't die in the process.

John tells us to test the spirits, but curiously, he doesn't really explain how we should do so. The examples cited in this chapter may appear extreme, but the people who became members of Heaven's

Gate, the Branch Davidians or Aum Shinri Kyo didn't think these groups were dangerous when they joined up. Nor did the hundreds of poor souls who committed mass suicide in 1978 at Jonestown, Jim Jones' authoritarian commune located in the jungles of Guyana.

Jesus provided some helpful advice in his comments on false prophets found in Matthew 7:15–18. "By their fruit you will recognize them." Like a shopper who goes to the grocery to get a melon, we must probe and test groups that claim to be speaking for God. A group may look fresh and shiny on the outside but check beneath the surface to see if members talk about abuse and authoritarianism.

Also be on the lookout for genetically modified fruits that claim to be better than the original. For example, some groups claim that no one has really understood the Bible for the past 20 centuries until their fearless leader arrived on the scene and explained it all for the first time. Watch out for charismatic leaders who offer novel explanations of the biblical passages. Such novelty got David Koresh and Jim Jones into deadly trouble, along with all their willing followers.

Believe in God, but don't follow every self-proclaimed prophet who claims he has the truth. What may appear beautiful might actually mask a horror beyond imagining.

————

Father, help me to test the spirits and to separate your truth from the spiritual falsehood that is so plentiful in the world.

93

God Knows Us Completely

Nothing in all creation is hidden from God's sight. Everything is uncovered and laid bare before the eyes of him to whom we must give account.

Hebrews 4:13

My (Lois) daughter Lara was never very good at covering up her wrongdoings. She couldn't bear the guilt and would turn herself in before I caught her.

I remember finding a note outside my bedroom door when she was about eleven years old that read, "Don't ask me what Mary and I did today at her house."

Now I know that isn't exactly a confession, but it certainly was an indication that she wanted to get a bad deed off her chest. As it turned out, she and Mary had watched a movie that I had forbidden Lara to see.

Often our sinful human natures cause us to automatically attempt to hide our faults or at least try to disguise our motives to reflect more innocence than we possess. How often have most of us re-peated a juicy piece of gossip wrapped in the guise of a prayer request, knowing that our motive was really to be the one who had the scoop on someone else? We love to see the shock on the face of our listener as we reveal privileged information.

It's a frightening thing to be completely uncovered before God, before the one "to whom we must give account."

Our salvation is not based on that account, but Scripture tells us that we will face judgment for rewards (1 Cor. 3:14) and suffer loss if our account is not pleasing to God. We won't suffer in heaven (Rev. 21:4), but we will stand before God on the day of judgment with all of our deeds exposed to him.

That truth is a powerful motivator to seek godliness in all aspects of our lives. God knows everything: not only what we do in secret but what we think, what we ponder in our hearts. His knowledge is not that of some cosmic killjoy, but rather the insight of a loving father who desires only the best for his children.

As his children we are disobedient and suffer the consequences. If we could hide from him, think how much more tempting it would be to do those things that cause us harm. Inability to hide from God is a good thing. It keeps us safe and helps us grow if we truly want to be the people he has called us to be.

My daughter knew as a little child that my restriction on her with regard to movies was for her own good. She faltered on at least that one occasion in obeying, but she did want me to know about it.

May we live in ways that desire God's watchful monitoring.

———

Father, sometimes we tremble to think that we cannot hide anything from you. Help us to live more and more in the light of your love, with no desire to avoid your loving eyes.

94

God's Standard of Beauty

But the LORD said to Samuel, "Do not consider his appearance or his height, for I have rejected him. The LORD does not look at the things man looks at. Man looks at the outward appearance, but the LORD looks at the heart."

1 Samuel 16:7

I WAS always tall for a girl, towering over the boys in my classes until about age fourteen. I hated it. My height also excluded me from being a serious ice-skater, something I would have loved, since the standard in that arena was "petite."

My parents enrolled me in modeling school to help improve my self-image, and it did the trick. I earned an astounding fifteen dollars an hour when modeling for local department stores, and people lauded me for my former nemesis—my height.

The emphasis on physical appearance that dominated many of my thoughts in my high school years continued over the decades right up to the present moment. I'm not alone. One of the prime audiences for cosmetic companies is the aging baby boomer generation. Ads claim remarkable results for faithful use of this or that cream. Plastic surgery and Botox treatments lure women my age into many a doctor's chair in attempts to cover up the aging process.

I am not critical of women who choose these procedures. I might consider it myself if I weren't such a wimp about pain. But in my heart of hearts I know that these superficial measures address an area of life that is a priority for the world and not a priority with God. God looks at the heart.

The power of this verse in 1 Samuel comes in the freedom it offers from this standard of perfection that surrounds us. If we can really grasp how God sees and values us, we escape from the damaging superficiality that can lead to poor self-esteem.

Another amazing reality this verse puts forth is that God looks at our hearts. He can see, even better than we can, what is the condition of our emotional and spiritual state.

How do we know what God sees when he looks deep inside of us? I think one of the most accurate ways to honestly evaluate our heart condition is to watch how we respond to life. An often-used test is how we drive a car and treat other drivers on the road. While this can be one measure, how we respond on the inside to many of life's circumstances may be a more accurate one.

Does my heart break when I watch the news or do I secretly wish others harm? Do I make opportunities to think well of someone whom I find irritating? Do I look at the world and other people with the eyes of Jesus?

Keeping a heart in godly condition is a constant challenge but so much more rewarding than a cleaned-up outside—tall or not—that harbors a run-down inside.

———

Father, thank you that you look at us inside and touch our lives to change our hearts.

95

Keep on Running

Therefore, since we are surrounded by such a great cloud of witnesses, let us throw off everything that hinders and the sin that so easily entangles, and let us run with perseverance the race marked out for us.

Hebrews 12:1

T HERE is a stadium. Runners are on the track at the starting line and the stands are full of cheering fans. At the beginning of the race, all the runners are energetic, fresh, and ready for the task ahead.

But this race is a long one. Soon the heat of the day and the length of the run begin to wear on the runners. Some of them become discouraged and fall behind the others. They have a long way to go and feel they cannot hang on. They are tempted to quit, to turn from the track and walk away from the contest.

Then the sound of the cheering fans breaks through their doubt. These particular fans hold great credibility for the runners: the onlookers have run this very race themselves. They endured to the end and now sit in the stands as a testament to those still running.

The fans wave and encourage the runners to look to the finish line. There in the distance a figure stands, tall and welcoming. He is clothed in white and his face shines brighter than the sun.

The runners and the fans know who this is. He is the "author and perfecter of [their] faith" (Heb. 12:2). Seeing him at the finish line in all his glory further inspires the runners to keep going. They know that they have suffered so little in comparison to the race he had to run. And he ran it on their behalf.

They run full of understanding and gratitude. Though their race is difficult, they are assured victory if they just don't quit. If they focus on Jesus and remain faithful to him, ever running toward him, they, too, will be victorious. They will receive "a harvest of righteousness and peace" (Heb. 12:11) and join the ranks of those in the stands who persevered to the end of their races.

We are the runners, those still alive here on earth who are called to "run with perseverance the race marked out for us." There is a gallery of runners that encourages us to keep on the path that follows Jesus. We can look to them and be empowered to persevere, even when our own race seems to be all uphill.

We are not running in the dark. The light of Jesus helps us stay on track and the knowledge that the ranks of heaven applaud us stirs us on.

We can remember believers who have gone before, endured hardships and now receive the reward of heaven. They did not turn away from God when life on this earth was difficult.

I remember one always-smiling saint, Charlie. It seemed that he led a charmed life. But his life had been touched deeply by grief, including the murder of his daughter. His explanation for his smile, even though life was painful, was that he "stayed under the spout where the blessings come out."

Charlie is in heaven now. Remembering his faith through fire gives me encouragement that we will be able to endure life's trials as well.

———

Father, when we are energized and encouraged our race seems easy, but when we tire and stumble it seems very long indeed. Help us to hear from heaven the throngs of those who have gone before us, and may their spiritual victories spur us on to crossing our own finish line.

96

Don't Worship God's Creation

And when you look up to the sky and see the sun, the moon and the stars—all the heavenly array—do not be enticed into bowing down to them and worshiping things the LORD your God has appointed to all the nations under heaven.

Deuteronomy 4:19

IRELAND'S first humans appeared there some ten thousand years ago. A few thousand years later, their descendants honored their dead by building massive stone tombs, many of them prominently placed on hilltops or other sacred places.

Newgrange is the most impressive of Ireland's hundreds of huge tombs. It is older than England's Stonehenge, and people celebrate it as one of the world's most amazing monuments.

A passageway leads to the center of a huge dirt mound and opens into a cross-shaped chamber area. During the winter solstice, the rising sun sends shafts of bright light streaming into the tomb through a small opening above the door, illuminating both the passageway and the inner burial chamber with a brilliant warm glow. This stunning light show lasts only seventeen minutes of one day every year.

While we don't know for certain the intent of the ancient builders of Newgrange, many believe that the tomb reveals how deeply those ancient people cared for the souls of the departed and revered the role of the sun in their lives.

I've gone to such detail here to illustrate the importance of nature to past civilizations. Deuteronomy 4:19, along with these ruins, attests to the powerful presence of God's creation. Spirituality today has once again embraced fascination with God's creation, but it often fails to acknowledge God as Creator. Alternative and New Age stores and catalogues entice customers to buy a wide range of goodies adorned with the sun, moon, and stars. Pagan spirituality includes ceremonies performed to the wonders of nature.

But God intended his creation to reflect him, not replace him. We need not fear enjoying God's creation or admiring people's monuments, but we must remember that anything other than God himself is not to be an object of worship.

———

Father, help us to enjoy fully the beauty you have created. Help us to be in awe of the wonders of your hand. And at the same time, keep us from adoring the work of the Creator instead of the Creator himself.

97

Just Do It

Do not merely listen to the word, and so deceive yourselves. Do what it says.

James 1:22

It has been one of the world's best-known advertising campaigns. Nike spent millions and millions of dollars hawking its athletic shoes and gear.

The company enlisted big-name celebrities such as Michael Jordan to endorse a series of ads that ended with the challenge: "Just do it."

The ads helped sell countless shoes and shorts and sweatpants. Even people who rarely moved a muscle purchased some of this gear. They wore their nice-looking athletic clothing only while sitting on the couch watching sports events on TV and snacking on chips and dip.

No matter how much athletic gear you buy, you'll never look like the muscular models in the ads unless you use it. And the same goes for those who practice the Christian faith.

James, the brother of Jesus, was a practical man. He had heard some of the leading early Christians promote lofty theological ideas. But for James, if Christianity didn't change one's life, it was all so much hot air. In his brief book, James repeatedly reminded his readers that Christianity is a faith of concrete action, not idle speculation.

If you say you are a Christian and you don't control your tongue, you are mistaken. If you say you love God but don't love your brother, you are deceived. If you say you have been saved by Christ but your life does not show the fruit of good works, you're kidding yourself.

Too often, we reduce Christianity to a pile of words. We assume that the people who can recite all the right theological terms know what they're doing. But sometimes action does not back up their words. "Preach always," said Saint Francis of Assisi. "If necessary, use words."

Saint Ignatius, who lived during the first century, was one of the earliest Christian leaders, serving as the bishop of Antioch. He would have agreed with Francis:

> It is better for a man to be silent and be [a Christian], than to talk and not to be one. It is good to teach, if he who speaks also acts. There is then one Teacher, who spake and it was done; while even those things which He did in silence are worthy of the Father.
>
> Let us therefore do all things as those who have Him dwelling in us, that we may be His temples, and He may be in us as our God, which indeed He is, and will manifest Himself before our faces. Wherefore we justly love Him.

Other saints from ages past confirm the message James gave us nearly twenty centuries ago: don't just listen to God's Word, but do what it says. Nike had the right idea: just do it. If you follow that advice, you'll be well on the way to being a better disciple of Jesus.

———

Father, help me convert my faith into action. Help me live out your Word in my daily life.

98

Wisdom or Knowledge?

Of making many books there is no end, and much study wearies the body.

> *Now all has been heard;*
> *here is the conclusion of the matter:*
> *Fear God and keep his commandments,*
> *for this is the whole duty of man.*

Ecclesiastes 12:12–13

OVER the last few decades, computers have gotten smaller, smarter, and faster. My first computer was a boxy machine with a small, monochrome monitor, limited memory, and processor speeds just slightly faster than the proverbial tortoise.

In the 1990s, hot new computers began talking to other computers over the worldwide Web. Soon, someone working at a desk in Timbuktu could download more data than a top-notch researcher could have tracked down a century before. And if you listened closely to some of the most optimistic predictions from evangelists of virtuality, computers would help people double the amount of information in the world every few years.

With all this progress, can world peace be far behind?

Solomon lived thousands of years ago. He never saw a computer, but he was pretty good with an abacus, and some people even say he was the wisest man who ever lived.

Solomon lived at a time when human knowledge was growing rapidly. Philosophers were probing the hidden nature of the cosmos and writing insightful books about politics and art. Solomon followed many of the important intellectual debates of his day. (The passage from Ecclesiastes indicates he experienced weariness along the way.)

He would have trouble grasping our modern-day computer revolution, but he was well familiar with people who confused wisdom with knowledge. Solomon's biblical Book of Proverbs is full of insightful comments about people who think they know everything but are actually fools.

Knowledge is information. It's the kind of thing you can look up with the help of a dictionary, encyclopedia, library card file, or Internet search engine. If you want to know how to build a nuclear bomb or a hospital, knowledge will help you do a better job.

It is wisdom, however, that helps you know whether a bomb or a hospital would be more helpful for the human race.

We are living in an information age. Advertisements tell us that there's more information on the computer chips in our digital camera or coffeemaker than there was in some of the world's biggest libraries a few centuries ago.

Half a dozen competing cable-TV news channels run nonstop chatter while across the bottom of the screen, breaking news bulletins, weather reports, and sports scores rapidly scroll by. Everywhere we turn, ads, sound bites, and promotions for this new product or that new service bombard us.

But as Solomon warned millennia ago, these things are not the source of the wisdom and guidance we need in life. No matter how much information we have, we still need the wisdom that comes only from God.

————

God, give me your wisdom so I can make my way through the information overload of modern life.

99

How the Mighty Are Fallen

Then they said, "Come, let us build ourselves a city, with a tower that reaches to the heavens, so that we may make a name for ourselves and not be scattered over the whole earth."

Genesis 11:4

WHEN a group of Middle Eastern terrorists decided to attack the United States, they chose a target that symbolized the nation's vast economic wealth and its pride in human accomplishment. In a matter of a few hours, the two huge World Trade Center towers—once the tallest structures in the world—crumbled into a mass of twisted metal and dust, taking nearly three thousand people to their deaths.

But the tragedy of September 11, 2001, wasn't the first time a tall tower symbolized people's pride in their accomplishments. Some four thousand years ago, a group of community leaders and hotshot executives from the booming ancient city of Babel decided to demonstrate how cool they were by building the world's first high-rise.

Here's how the New Living Translation (NIT) of the Bible renders the verse from Genesis: "Let's build a great city with a tower that reaches to the skies—a monument to our greatness!"

The proposed project was a great unifier for the city of Babel. People contributed raw materials and labor to the project. And as the tower rose into the sky, the citizens of Babel began to feel pretty proud of themselves.

God wasn't too excited about their plans, which they designed to unify all of the people of the world into one common language. "Just think of what they'll do later," he said. "Nothing will be impossible for them!" (Gen. 11:6 NIT)

God scattered the people from the plains of Babylonia, sending them all over the world and giving them many different languages that would complicate future building efforts.

It's not that God doesn't like big buildings. After all, when God created humanity in his image, he gave us the ability to create enormous, wonderful projects. And God isn't upset when people talk to one another. He gave us our minds and our mouths.

What did bother God was the fact that people didn't consult him before cooking up a plan to promote world harmony by secular means. The people of Babel wanted to demonstrate their own greatness by building a tower to the sky. They were so arrogant that they thought their tower could prevent their being "scattered over the whole earth" and instead lead to their greater unification.

Similar promises have been made about technological developments throughout human history. The transatlantic cable was supposed to bring the world together. And the Internet would make us all smarter and tear down barriers between countries!

God loves it when people use the talents and skills he has given them to make the world a better place. But before you build a monument to your own greatness—any symbol of pride and accomplishment—stop and consult God about your plans. He might have a better idea.

———

God, thank you for giving people tremendous gifts and abilities. But help us to serve you with our talents rather than trying to create a secular utopia on our own.

100

Taking Time Out for God

Be still, and know that I am God.

Psalm 46:10

A FEW years ago Steve and I were enjoying a vacation in Europe with another couple. Our first stop was Paris, which is a bustling whirl of activity day and night. We filled every moment of our four days there.

On the fifth morning we headed for Switzerland. Our bed-and-breakfast near Geneva overlooked the lake. We oohed and aahed at the sight of such peaceful surroundings after the hustle of Paris. But sighs of delight had barely escaped my lips when I shifted gears. "I'm off!" I announced.

It was around 1:00 P.M. when I walked expectantly down the hill and toward the main street of the town. I noticed that the streets were relatively deserted.

A sign on the door of the first shop I approached explained the lack of foot traffic: "Closed from noon until three." I tried the doorknob anyway, but it was locked. I jiggled it as if there were some mistake. Frustrated, I went to the next shop. The same sign in the store window was embroidered in needlepoint, but I didn't appreciate the artistic touch.

I walked back to the hotel to snatch Steve from whatever cozy chair he had settled into, only to find him in our room asleep. Our friends were nowhere to be found, and I could only assume that they, too, were resting.

I didn't want to sleep! I didn't want to read! I wanted to be out and about, doing something!

With an irritated sigh, I finally sat in one of the chairs in the library off to the left of the entrance to the B & B. I put my feet up on an ottoman and laid my head back.

One of my favorite Rachmaninoff melodies was lilting from the CD player. I realized that the stillness was pleasant. The tension in my body began to drain away. The breeze from the lake drifted through the open French doors and carried with it the scent of lilac. *Why don't I do this more often?* I asked myself.

There was an almost audible response: *You are addicted to busyness.*

I really felt that I had heard God speak to me. In the stillness he impressed upon me my need to heed the words of Psalm 46:10.

Virtually everyone I know struggles with the curse of busyness. We live in a culture that thrives on action, always moving, doing more, accomplishing more. It's no wonder that God sometimes seems far away or difficult to understand. Our minds are so full of many thoughts about our busy schedules that we miss his still, small voice.

My afternoon in Switzerland showed me how refreshed I could be if I just paced myself with time to be in God's presence. It's still a challenge, but now I have more stillness in my life than I did before.

Father, help us to experience the peaceful fullness of resting in your presence.

101

A Welcome Return

He who testifies to these things says, "Yes, I am coming soon."
Amen. Come, Lord Jesus.

Revelation 22:20

WHEN I was a little girl my father did a lot of traveling for his job. Sometimes he would be gone for weeks at a time, and my mother and I would carry on with life together.

As the time drew near for him to return, I'd start to count the days. When *the* day arrived, I peered out the living room window, eager to see his car pull up in front of our house. He was tall and lean and took the front steps in great strides, calling my name as he ran into the house.

I always charged into his arms before he could reach the front door. He'd scoop me up and hug me tight. I felt secure and loved and so very glad that he was home.

Now I am a grandmother and have the opportunity to see my grandchildren anticipate and greet their fathers at the end of each day. When I am with Lara and family in California for example, the sound of the garage door ignites the children's excitement. "Daddy's home!" Lisa yells and dances in place. The twins immediately drop the toys that so fascinated them just minutes before and run to the door. All three run and throw themselves into Daddy's encircling arms. Craig scoops them up and warmly hugs them close to him.

This young father is gone only during the course of each day. And yet his children look forward to their father's return with great anticipation. Their father is a safe, loving, and godly reflection of their Father in heaven.

Jesus tells us that he will be coming back. He will usher in a new age and will reign over all the earth. He will defeat evil.

Even so, we sometimes don't anticipate his return as we might. I think it is because we know this world and the next world is unknown. We want to raise our families and enjoy the fruits of our labor. But if we could only glimpse the delight that will be ours when he returns, we might be more excited.

When Lara was little she used to look at the sun filtering down through clouds, creating a fanlike display of shimmering light. She'd excitedly say, "Look! Maybe Jesus is coming back today!"

Her childish wonder was wonderful. She looked with anticipation to the day when Jesus would come back and claim his own.

There are a multitude of questions about the coming of Christ and what will happen afterward that we can't answer. But we can enjoy the anticipation of his return, like a little child delighted to see Daddy walk through the door.

————

Father, thank you that one day all will be well. One day Jesus will return to claim his own. We look forward to that day.

Notes

Chapter 4

1. Quotes from Saint Bernard of Clairvaux are from *On Loving God* taken from *The Master Christian Library CD-ROM* (Rio, Wis.: Ages Software, 1998).

Chapter 7

1. St. Francis quotes from Marion A. Habig, editor, *St. Francis of Assisi: Writings and Early Biographies* (Quincy, Ill.: Franciscan Press, 1991).

Chapter 11

1. C. S. Lewis, *The Joyful Christian* (New York: Macmillan, 1977), pp. 127–128.
2. Ibid., p. 11.

Chapter 35

1. Dana Carvey quotes from Steve Rabey, "A Chat with the Church Lady," *The Magazine for Christian Youth!* July 1988, pp. 20–21.

Chapter 37

1. Robert Barron, *Heaven in Stone and Glass: Experiencing the Spirituality of Great Cathedrals* (New York: Crossroad, 2000), p. 12.

Chapter 38

1. Dietrich Bonhoeffer, *The Cost of Discipleship* (New York: Macmillan, 1963), p. 7. All other Bonhoeffer quotes in chapter are from pages 47–48.

Chapter 56

1. Wade Clark Roof, *A Generation of Seekers: The Spiritual Journeys of the Baby Boom Generation* (San Francisco: HarperSanFrancisco, 1993), p. 22.

Chapter 62

1. Frederick Buechner, *Wishful Thinking* (New York: Harper & Row, 1973), pp. 88–89.
2. Ibid.

Chapter 92

1. Heaven's Gate quotes from Elizabeth Gleick, "The Marker We've Been Waiting For," *Time*, April 7, 1997, pp. 29–36.